Reframing Your Ministry

Balancing Professional Responsibilities & Personal Needs

Anthony J. Headley, Ph.D.

Evangel
Publishing House

Nappanee, Indiana 46550

Requests for information should be addressed to:
Evangel Publishing House
2000 Evangel Way
P.O. Box 189
Nappanee, Indiana 46550
Phone: (800) 253-9315
Internet: www.evangelpublishing.com

Cover Design by Jeffrey Hall, ION Graphic Design Works
Edited by Mark Garratt

ISBN-13: 978-1-928915-97-3
ISBN-10: 1-928915-97-3
Library of Congress Control Number: 2007934661

Printed in the United States of America

13 14 15 16 17 EP 8 7 6 5 4 3 2

To my father, Charles

Table of Contents

Introduction

"Minister thought dead, discovered alive in California!" This true story never made the headlines, although it probably should have! Feeling overwhelmed by the stresses of ministry, this minister abandoned everything—his wife, his children, his home and his congregation. He drove down to the local river, carefully placed his shoes on the bank, and disappeared. Naturally, everyone thought he had committed suicide. A service was held in his memory, and his family and congregation tried to move on. A few years later, however, a former church member boarding a bus on the West Coast came face to face with his supposedly dead pastor!

What an incredible story! In fact, I always thought it somewhat incredulous until one minister personally related to me a similar tale. While he didn't go so far as to fake his own death, he did abandon his spouse and children for nearly two years because he felt overwhelmed by the pressures of ministry.

What leads ministers to take such drastic measures? Although I am not so naïve to believe that ministry life is the only source of stress, I have no doubt that its seemingly unrelenting people- and time-related demands serve as major triggers. But, you may say, these demands are faced daily by ministers everywhere, and not every pastor's career goes down in flames. This is true. But if the weighty responsibilities of Christian service are not to blame when burnout does occur, something else is. I contend that the "something else" is *the way we think about and practice ministry*. If we begin with the false premise that ministry is simply what is done with and for others, we set in motion a maddening behavioral style obsessed with doing. In a sense, it's like wearing blinders. Seeing only the myriad needs of others in the church and community, we can become blind to our own needs and those of our family to the neglect of health and well-being.

In short, life can get out of balance. This is why we need to rethink, or reframe, ministry. It is also why I have written this book. Our attitudes toward ministry are often ingrained and changing them is no easy task. Moreover, there are many in the body of Christ who would consider it heresy to speak of reserving a primary place for serving self and family. To them it sounds like a selfish endeavor. Nothing could be further from the truth! Jesus taught that we must love our neighbors *as ourselves*. As pastors and professionals, we must embrace this mature view of our role, taking our cues from Scripture, not from the voices of habit and self-imposed guilt. It is my passion and prayer that you find in these pages the key to long-term ministry success: a love for God that encompasses both self-care and care for others.

Dr. Tony Headley
Wilmore, Kentucky

Chapter 1

Reframing Ministry

The Stresses of Ministry

There's no getting around it. Ministry is stressful. One minister succinctly captured the multi-faceted images of stress in this poignant piece:

> If I wanted to drive a manager up the wall, I would make him responsible for the success of an organization and give him no authority. I would provide him with unclear goals, not commonly agreed upon by the organization. I would ask him to provide a service of an ill-defined nature, apply a body of knowledge having few absolutes, and staff his organization with only volunteers. I would expect him to work ten to twelve hours per day and have his work evaluated by a committee of 300 to 500 amateurs. I would call him a minister and make him accountable to God.[1]

It's hard to miss the screaming frustration embedded in these words. We could dismiss them as the pain of one sarcastic pastor. But this minister mirrors pastoral reality. Unfortunately, he paints a very accurate picture of many ministers' plight. Most ministers who have served for any length of time probably shouted a loud amen at the images his words evoked. Within his statement I hear several stresses which characterize clergy work.

Ministers often struggle with *a sense of responsibility without authority (and often without resources or gratitude)*. Pastors often shoulder responsibility for their own and other people's performance. Parishioners expect clergy to respond ably to the church's problems. At the same time they must sometimes cope with difficult and angry volunteers. In spite of these expectations, the necessary authority and resources are, at times, withheld or grudgingly given. A rigidly entrenched power structure allows little place for pastors to meaningfully influence the church's direction. Sometimes, the power and resources necessary for making change largely reside in the hands of powerful others in the church. Though some might say ministers ultimately derive their authority from God, they often serve in situations where church leaders hold tight reins on power and control. In this situation, ministers become little more than hired hands, possessing no real power to enact needed change. Without the necessary resources, the weight of responsibility contributes to role overload and frustration within the pastor's life.

Some ministers labor in churches with *unclear organizational values and goals.* There are few, if any, agreed-upon goals, norms, philosophies or ideologies to guide them. I once read of a church possessing no bylaws for its governance. A few powerful lay leaders had monopolized control, making up the rules as they went along. They were most apt to do this when their control seemed threatened. This church had many problems. No wonder! Without organizational clarity, real progress is impossible. Struggles, conflict and stress naturally ensue. Working in such an organization is like being on a ship in a tumultuous ocean without a rudder or a compass. Such an organization is doomed to spin aimlessly. That's why many organizations now craft mission statements. These statements define for members the values and goals of the organization. Unfortunately, many churches function without such purpose and vision. This is evidently part of the problem highlighted in the pastor's words.

Given the lack of organizational clarity and direction, the problem of *unclear and ambiguous expectations* makes perfect sense. If a business lacks explicit goals and direction, it's often fuzzy about what its employees should do. This is often the case in pastoral settings. Over and over again, writers on clergy stress highlight this problem.[2] In my own research and conversations with pastors, this has shown up as a critical issue. Sometimes ministers complain that they don't know their role expectations and how they should spend their time. Usually they also lack clarity about the evaluation criteria by which they will be judged and what they need to do to make progress.

As if role ambiguity was not bad enough, the minister may *"...have his work evaluated by a committee of 300 to 500 amateurs."* Without clear organizational goals, what criteria will these amateurs use? Simple! Those which each parishioner deems important! The result is 300 to 500 committees of one, each with definitive expectations of the pastor. In addition, each church board, committee and denominational agency may lay out different priority expectations. So, the minister finds himself trying desperately to meet multiple demands from varied quarters. These people mean well, but there's no mutual agreement about the expectations. And even if they do agree, it is doubtful a minister could actually live with the expectations and still be human. Such a person would have to conform to the following description of the perfect minister I encountered in a church magazine:

> After hundreds of years, a model preacher has been found to suit everyone. He preaches exactly 20 minutes and then sits down. He condemns sins but never hurts anyone.
>
> He works from 8:00 a.m. to 10:00 p.m. in every type of work from preaching to custodial services. He makes $60.00 a week, wears good clothes, buys books regularly, has a nice family, drives a good car and gives $30.00 a week to the church. He also stands ready to contribute to every good work that comes along.
>
> He is 26 years old and has been preaching for 30 years. He is tall and short, thin and heavyset, and handsome. He has one brown eye and one blue; hair parted in the middle; left side, dark and straight; the right side, brown and wavy.
>
> He has a burning desire to work with teenagers and spends all his time with older folk. He smiles all the time with a straight face because he has a sense of humor that keeps him seriously dedicated to his work.
>
> He makes 15 calls a day on the church members, spends all his time evangelizing the unchurched, and is never out of his office.[3]

The disgruntled pastor's statement also highlights the stress experienced when the church *functions without absolutes.* Unfortunately, we live at a time when tolerance has become a cultural norm and mandate. Anyone who dares speak about absolutes risks being branded a bigot. In some quarters, the church has succumbed to this cultural peer pressure. Instead of a constant message, the church sometimes opts for shifting standards of truth—*"a body of knowledge having few absolutes."* Many churches are guided by rules of pluralism and relativism where almost anything is tolerated. This stance creates a great degree of uncertainty about the organizational philosophy and direction.

Recently, a frustrated pastor shared with me his experience serving a church desiring tolerance at any price. He was roundly criticized for preaching common biblical doctrines like sin and forgiveness. In one meeting, church leaders actually asked him not to preach these unaccustomed themes. They feared such biblical absolutes would alienate persons who came to the church. Eventually, some of these leaders became disgruntled enough to leave the church. This inevitably created a great deal of short-term conflict and stress both for the pastor and those who remained. I have also encountered several ministers who struggled when the church shied away from any talk of absolutes. Some became frustrated enough to leave the organization or give up ministry altogether.

Which pastor out there doesn't understand the problems involved when one must *"...staff his organization with only volunteers?"* Yet ministers do this every day. And if we are honest, it's part of God's design. But uncommitted volunteers can cause trouble. Much of the time they may prove unreliable. Since they do not serve for pay, motivation may flag. Sometimes they quit their responsibilities at the slightest show of conflict, even in the middle of an important project. This often leaves ministers scrambling to find replacements. Such is the plight of anyone who works with volunteers.

There is a common misconception that ministers work very few hours. In reality, they often work long hours, being available 24-7. When the pastor sarcastically stated, *"I would expect him to work ten to twelve hours per day,"* he wasn't necessarily exaggerating. A 1991 study by the Fuller Institute of Church

Growth found 90% of pastors worked more than 46 hours per week.[4] This is paltry compared to the working hours of some pastors I have encountered. One "successful" pastor spoke about working 100 hours per week. More astounding, the two other ministers with whom he met for accountability put in well over 110 hours. One wonders how well they held each other accountable. Such horrendous hours dehumanize the pastor. The pastor's physical, emotional and family health slides down the priority list.

The last sentence, *"I would call him a minister and make him accountable to God,"* suggests to me a kind of spiritual guilt making. I don't mean to suggest that pastors aren't accountable to God. They are. But sometimes people in the pew use this commitment and accountability to God as a spiritual club to provoke false guilt. As a result, a minister might end up in a classic double bind. The job is so stressful, so multi-faceted and ambiguous, one person could not possibly do it. At the same time, the minister cannot leave the job because account must ultimately be given to God. And of course, God doesn't like quitters. So the minister is trapped, finding it unbearable to stay, but also impossible to leave, lest the fury of a deity who is a hard taskmaster be unleashed. This view of God is a mistaken one, but it works nonetheless. The minister caught in this predicament might remain, but sinks down into quiet despair—without fire and without passion.

The Need for Reframe

The pastor we met at the beginning of the chapter clearly reveals the heart of ministry stress. But he does more. Whether intentional or not, his words betray a certain understanding of ministry. He frames ministry as *management*, albeit in a dysfunctional organization. What's more, his ministry mindset seems like one largely framed by others and over which the minister feels little if any control. It also seems outwardly focused in that it concerns itself with crushing expectations which allow no place for personal well-being. In my opinion, a great deal of ministry stress springs from this sort of misunderstanding. How we frame ministry has an awful lot to do with the amount of stress we experience. If we work out of one-sided, inadequate models, we give rise to a behavioral style which exacerbates stress. Once we have bought into this erroneous understanding, some of the stresses discussed above are virtually inevitable. Thomas Oden comes to a similar conclusion. He indicates that a major cause of burnout derives from "the blurring of pastoral identity." By this he means that there is confusion about the nature of ministry. Furthermore, he indicates that burnout complications could be avoided if conceptions of ministry were built on better biblical foundations.[5] From my perspective, Oden is speaking about the need for reframing ministry.

Such a misconceived understanding of ministry would not be a problem if it was an isolated one. But it is not. Instead, this other-centered perspective is widespread. In clergy seminars I often try to discern pastors' understanding of ministry. I often ask them, "What is ministry?" I assume their answers would reflect their working understanding. If this is true then there is a real problem. Invariably (my guess would be 99 percent of the time) they answer, "Ministry is what you do for others," or some similar response. Rarely do they include self-care and family care in their definition. No wonder ministers perform so horribly in these critical care areas. It's because they do not believe they perform ministry when they attend to these needs! To do ministry they think they must constantly serve others to the neglect of themselves and their loved ones.

Pastors are not the only ones who endorse this misunderstanding. Church leaders sometimes fall into the same error. Much of the time their misconception of ministry flows out of their own stories and history. They have functioned out of misperceived models of ministry and expect ministers under their charge to do the same. Furthermore, some leaders embrace a corporate model which asks employees to sell their souls for the company's good. One of my former seminary professors said to me, "They [church leaders] run the church like IBM, don't they?" This is not to demean sound leadership and business strategies. God knows we need it! But sometimes leaders see numbers and growth as the bottom line. Their chief priority is to ensure the church's growth and meet parishioners' needs. In short, they seek the things which implicitly demand an other-centered approach to ministry. They can become so focused on these ends they may not see the heavy personal and family price ministers pay. I do not mean to suggest that they are callous to the needs of ministers. I only suggest their primary focus tends to overshadow the minister's personal needs. Not surprisingly, the minister's needs get lost in the shuffle.

I saw this phenomenon in a doctor of ministry dissertation. The researcher asked denominational leaders to reflect on the mentoring needs of new ministers. These leaders rated professional needs as the chief concern for new pastors, followed by personal and spiritual needs. When these same leaders described the top ten needs of new pastors, seven of the ten related to professional needs. These included areas such as working with problem people, providing encouragement and support, resolving conflict, vision casting and initiating change. In contrast, when the researcher asked the same questions of pastors, they primarily spoke of their needs in spiritual terms. In fact, six of their top ten needs fell into this category. New pastors highlighted needs such as cultivating their inner life, developing accountability relationships, a vital prayer life, spiritual disciplines and living a holy life.[6] The two responding groups were worlds apart in their perceptions. I suspect the church leaders' perspective flowed from an other-centered understanding of ministry. For them, ministers should primarily focus on the well-being of others and facilitate the church's growth.

Many church members also misunderstand ministry. Borrowing clergy's error, they assume ministers ought to spend all their time meeting parishioners' needs. Some may even resent it when ministers and their families appear to be human persons encumbered with needs, including the need for time to themselves. Compounding this problem is a related misunderstanding: only ordained and vocational ministers can do ministry. This excludes a large part of the church from actual involvement in ministry and inevitably compounds the demands and the stress on clergy.

This is why I suggest a new (actually, rediscovered) understanding of ministry is needed. A more accurate understanding will free us to pursue ministry in a different style. New perspectives tend to breed new behaviors. We often change our habits because we have first changed our thinking. One church leader illustrated this for me. We sat next to each other during the lunch break of a clergy gathering. A conversation about ministry ensued. He recounted how he spent his early years in ministry driven by workaholic tendencies. Even his young child noticed his approach and suggested that his workaholic style was destroying him. Now with age and maturity, he had arrived at a new understanding of ministry. This new perspective freed him from workaholic tendencies and permitted a balanced approach to ministry.

One of my clergy friends also confirmed this. We had attended Bible college together and I remembered him as a joyous fellow who loved nothing better than going to the beach. A few years ago, he was in a clergy self-care seminar I led. I later learned that doing ministry had led him to give up some simple pleasures. Fear and a misplaced sense of guilt plagued him. He feared that if he took time to address his recreational and health needs, his congregation would think of him as lazy. He also experienced feelings of guilt when he took the time to do something recreational. At that time, I assured him that self-care *was* ministry.

Sometime later, I had a chance to speak with him. I wanted to know how he was coping with ministry stress. Thankfully, he was coping better. Something from the seminar had taken hold. He now cared more diligently for himself. In fact, when I spoke to him he was vacationing. I was curious to discover what part of the seminar had precipitated his change. Was it the understanding of how stress works? Was it the emphasis on self-care strategies? What had freed him from the fear and false guilt that previously shackled him? It was the idea of self-care as ministry. That discovery had freed him from his bondage. It had set him back on a path to personal well-being.

I have heard similar comments from other ministers. Unfortunately, most arrive at this understanding much later in life. Sometimes it only comes after some ministry crisis compels them to find a different style of doing ministry. Sometimes it comes because of personal or family tragedy. All this convinces me of the need to take a fresh look at ministry to understand its true meaning. Ministry needs to be framed in ways that make it consistent with the well-being of clergy as well as people in the pew. In short, ministry needs to be reframed.

The Meaning of Reframe
Changing Thinking, Feelings and Actions

What do I mean by reframe? Up to this point I have only hinted at its meaning. I now wish to define this term and explore its applications to ministry. An illustration of its meaning might be a good place to begin. Sometime ago, I ate lunch at an area restaurant. As I prepared to leave, I met an elderly couple entering. The old gentleman held the door open for his wife. As he paused at the door, I couldn't help noticing the words splashed across the baseball cap he wore: *"Aged to Perfection."* This old fellow was making a statement. He was declaring something about himself and his age. For him, age did not mean *deterioration*, it meant *enhancement*. Age meant perfection. This is a wonderful example of reframe.

Reframe simply means to put a situation or concept in a new light. In the book Change, the authors define reframe in the following language: "...to change the conceptual and/or emotional setting or viewpoint in relation to which a situation is experienced and to place it in another frame which fits the 'facts' of the same concrete situation equally well or even better and thereby change its entire meaning."[7] In *Reframing Organizations*, Bolman and Deal declare: "Frames are both windows on the world and lenses that bring the world into focus. Frames filter out some things while allowing others to pass through easily. Frames help us order experience and decide what to do. Every manager, consultant, or policymaker relies on a personal frame or image to gather information, make judgments and determine how to best get things done."[8]

From these definitions we learn a few things about reframe. It involves changing how one views a situation or concept. This essentially changes the meaning even if objective circumstances remain the same. This type of change involves shifts in perception and meaning. Sometimes we experience problems because we begin with a faulty understanding. Our information about the facts may be fuzzy and out of focus. That is, we are not viewing things as clearly as we should. It's as though we see through a glass darkly. We are like the blind man of Bethsaida who, touched once by Jesus, saw men as trees walking. He needed a second touch to bring him to clear sight; to see men as they really are, not trees, but living, breathing persons (Mark 8:22-26). Reframe is like that. It's like a second touch that sheds light on fuzzy stuff. It more clearly reveals what was once obscured, hidden or unknown. Once the situation is cast in a different light, obscured truth is revealed.

But reframe involves more than just the head. It does more than just change the way a person *thinks*. It also changes the way the individual *feels*. It actually shifts emotions. A good example can be drawn from counseling with those who have experienced trauma. In some cases, the memories of their trauma remain dormant for a long time. When memories return, some persons are distraught. They often think they are weak. For them, their weakness causes these painful memories to return. Sometimes a positive reframe can put the situation in a different light. Rather than weak, one might suggest that they are finally strong enough to face the pain. That's why God has allowed the painful memories to break through. This doesn't change the pain, but casts it in a different light. It helps them think differently about themselves. They are not weak. They are finally strong enough to bear the pain and work through it. It also casts a different light on their feelings about God. He has not abandoned them, but is actually with them in the midst of their pain. Rather than feeling rejected, they may feel supported and loved by God.

Sometimes changing the emotional viewpoint means making a negative reframe. For example, workaholic ministers often "sanctify" their style by framing it as sacrificial service. Like political spin-doctors they try to put a positive meaning to their destructive tendencies. In these cases it may be necessary to "spit in their soup," to cast their behavior in a negative light. This might involve framing their workaholic behavior as springing from their need for attention. They may continue their habits, but now they must also deal with the thought that this habit springs not from a spiritual source, but from this overwhelming need. Over time, this "tainted soup" may not taste quite as good. In fact, this change in viewpoint may force them to face their tremendous need for attention and may contribute to a shift in how they feel about and perform ministry. Ultimately, reframe possesses the power to change behavior. The minister who begins to redefine "sacrificial ministry" as attention-getting behavior may make concerted efforts to change. *Thinking differently* and *feeling differently* almost always seem to contribute to *acting differently*.

Mark Twain's *Tom Sawyer* provides an excellent example of these features of reframe. The example occurs near the beginning of the book. For the umpteenth time, Tom had incurred the wrath of Aunt Polly. She sentenced him to whitewash thirty yards of board fence nine feet high. As a result, on a bright and glorious Saturday morning, while boys frolicked at the local watering hole, Tom began his sentence. At that moment his life seemed hollow and burdensome. What's more, Tom dreaded the taunting he would be sure to receive from boys passing by. Most of all, he dreaded the taunts of Ben Rogers. As if his punishment was not already burdensome enough, who should appear but the dreaded Ben! But Tom had a magnificent inspiration in this dark moment of need. Moved by this inspiration, he took his brush and went to work. As Ben came near, Tom ignored his presence and continued his work. Like a masterful artist, he occasionally paused and stepped back to survey the effect of his brushstrokes. The following conversation soon ensued:

"Hello, old chap, you got to work, hey?"

Tom wheeled suddenly and said,

"Why, it's you, Ben! I warn't noticing."

"Say—I'm going a-swimming, I am. Don't you wish you could? But of course you'd druther *work*—wouldn't you? Course you would!"

Tom contemplated the boy a bit, and said,

"What do you call work?"

"Why, ain't *that* work?"

Tom resumed his whitewashing, and answered carelessly,

"Well, maybe it is, and maybe it ain't. All I know is, it suits Tom Sawyer."

"Oh, come now, you don't mean to let on that you *like* it?"

The brush continued to move.

"Like it? Well, I don't see why I oughtn't to like it. Does a boy get a chance to whitewash a fence everyday?"

That put the thing in a new light [Italics mine]. Ben stopped nibbling his apple. Tom swept his brush daintily back and forth—stepped back to note the effect—added a touch here and there—criticized the effect again—Ben watching every move and getting more and more interested, more and more absorbed. Presently he said:

"Say, Tom, let *me* whitewash a little."[9]

Tom had cleverly reframed his work. He now portrayed the dreaded task, not as drudgery, but a *once-in-a-lifetime privilege*. Certainly no boy could resist such an opportunity! We all know Tom's reframe was a cleverly devised plan to avoid work. However, one should not miss the power of the reframe on Ben. He saw whitewashing the fence in a new light—a chance of a lifetime. Once he made that cognitive shift, he began to have different feelings about the task. This was not something to dread—a task to keep a boy from a Saturday morning swim. Rather, it was something to enjoy—a task to covet and savor. Eventually, thought and emotions led to desire and action. Thus, we have the request: "Say, Tom, let me whitewash a little." Tom, a retired artist turned entrepreneur, would spend the day amassing wealth. The neighborhood boys happily surrendered their material possessions for the high privilege of whitewashing a fence! They came to jeer, but fell under the power of Tom's reframe and joyously stayed to whitewash. That's the ultimate power of reframe. It changes behavior!

The Power to Change Systems

Reframe also possesses the power to change a whole system. Some call this *second-order change*. That's intended to contrast it with *first-order change* in which the system remains the same. An example from ministry should provide greater clarity and distinction between first-order and second-order change. Let's say that, in a given church, needs and demands have increased.

First-order change might involve a demand for the minister to do more to meet those needs. Nothing changes but the pastor's workload. If there are sufficient monetary resources, the church might even hire a pastoral assistant. In this second scenario, the size of the church's staff might change, but the system remains essentially the same. They remain stuck in the same rut regarding ministry: *ministry involves work done by professionals*. That's an example of first-order change. A few things might change, but the church's systemic beliefs and practices remain the same.

But let's suppose something happens in the congregation. That event (often a crisis) helps the congregation reframe ministry as something done by all of God's people. If everyone enters into this reframe, then the whole system, ministers and congregation, changes. Both the leaders and the people become involved in serving to the benefit of pastor and parishioners. That's second-order change—change that affects the whole church system. Reframing ministry could bring about this fundamental shift in the whole church.

Doing Justice to the Facts

A good reframe always does justice to the facts. In making a reframe, the worst thing one can do is to craft one grossly out of touch with the way things really are. These ill-advised efforts possess no power or life and are easily dismissed. The effective reframe stays close to the facts. It simply arranges the data in a different way, thus creating a new picture. The picture was there all along, but because of the way the facts were arranged or distorted, the picture was blurred, hidden and unseen.

A reframe also serves to filter information. It helps to keep the good in and the garbage out. Sometimes much of our knowledge, based as it is on false information and false premises, is like garbage which contributes to emotional and behavioral turmoil. A reframe seeks to keep what is good while filtering out what is garbage; it keeps the baby but throws out the bath water. In this regard, it guides judgments, decisions and action. It helps us sort through a variety of facts and judge their validity. Having worked our way through a tangled jumble of facts, we can more clearly perceive our options and come to the most appropriate course of action. In addition, reframing situations actually helps us determine our priorities.

The ability to reframe is a tremendous asset to leaders. Bolman and Deal suggest that reframe can enrich and broaden a leader's repertoire. In addition, it can serve as a powerful antidote to self-entrapment. This is partly true because reframe helps leaders to generate creative responses to the challenges they face.[10] Reframing can serve as a powerful tool for good. On the other hand, failing to frame a situation accurately can have devastating consequences.

In *Reframing Organizations*, the authors provide a powerful illustration of the negative consequences of inaccurate framing. They recount the story of the crew of a jetliner which had taken off from New York City. Apparently, the crew noticed they were having high air speed readouts. Puzzled, they attributed the readouts to unusual updrafts. They couldn't have been more wrong. They had actually failed to turn on the heaters which prevent freeze-up in the air speed indicators. Having misread the situation, they thought they were approaching the speed of sound and needed to slow down. To rectify the situation, the pilot kept easing back on the throttle. Instead, it placed them in danger of an engine stall. They eventually realized the error but, by then, the aircraft was plunging to the ground, out of control. Both plane and crew were destroyed. The authors conclude: "...the costs of misreading a situation can be dire—in an airplane, a business or government."[11] The same truth applies to ministry. Misreading ministry can lead to dire consequences. The many stories of ministry stress and burnout provide strong testimony to the negative consequences that ensue when we fail to frame ministry accurately.

Reframing Ministry
Older Is Wiser

Older and wiser ministers may already serve from reframed understandings of ministry. Consistently in the literature, older ministers do better with stress and burnout than younger ministers. I suspect a large part of this difference springs from two sources. First, older ministers learned from their initial errors and found ways to work smarter rather than harder. Second, older ministers became wiser and used that wisdom to craft a more personally benevolent view of ministry; they found new models which allowed them to show more self-compassion.

Other ministers are finding ways to shift their understanding. In an edition of the journal, *Leadership*, one minister demonstrated the difference reframing makes. He moved from understanding ministry as crisis management to providing spiritual direction. This reframe liberated him and four other pastors from a co-dependent relationship with a congregation of 9,500 people. What led him to this redefinition of ministry? He discovered that the Apostle Paul had focused more on spiritual direction than pastoral care. In the process he made a simple discovery and shared it with his congregation: *"There is no way that in a church of 9,500 members that five pastors can be present for every spiritual event in your lives. You will have a crisis, and we will do everything we can to equip you to face it."*[12] And they did. They developed care networks to which members could go. Now, in times of crisis, members seek support from their care groups rather than the pastoral staff. This pastor had reframed his understanding of ministry and, in the process, reformed both his practice and an entire congregation. This change in style translated into more effective ministry in the congregation and, concomitantly, the lightening of pastoral burdens.

I found a similar example in an interview conducted with Eugene Peterson, author of *The Message*. Peterson recalled a time in his ministry when, according to him, he deviated from the center. Those were the times when he tried to meet people's needs on their terms. As a result, he spent an inordinate amount of time in marriage counseling and various other forms of ministry—all to make the church successful.[13] These things were important, but when they came to define his pastoral work, he found he had deviated from the center. What's the center of pastoral work for Peterson? For him, "The most important thing a pastor does is to stand in the pulpit every Sunday and say, 'Let us worship God.' If that ceases to be the primary thing I do in terms of my energy, my imagination and the way I structure my life, then I no longer function as a pastor. I pick up some other identity."[14]

Peterson obviously developed a new frame for conducting ministry. That new window on ministry framed it as saint-making achieved through worship. That's a far cry from framing ministry as fulfilling human potential or ministry as management. In turn, this reframe informed his practices. That frame apparently had an awful lot to do with how he used his energy and structured his life. I suspect such a frame meant finding more time to be with God. Desiring to bring people into God's presence, he had to abide in that presence himself.

Back to the Book

These illustrations give excellent insight into what a new frame would mean for pastoral practice. First, it would mean *a rediscovered understanding of the nature and practice of ministry.* Rather than solely an other-centered activity, ministry would become more fully orbed and capable of serving the well-being of both minister and parishioner. It would also mean pausing to take a fresh look at the facts surrounding ministry. Thus, we would see aspects of ministry that have been clouded over and darkened by years of misunderstandings.

Where would we go to find such facts? I suggest we can locate these facts in our ultimate source, the Bible. The Bible is replete with data supporting a more balanced understanding of ministry. This biblical perspective is shared by many classic writers in the church.[15] Furthermore, I contend that the understanding I propose does greater justice to the biblical data on ministry than the other-centered model commonly proposed and practiced. We will cover some of those biblical passages in the chapters that follow. Particularly, we will investigate two models for doing ministry. In chapters 2–5, we will look at the primary model that informs many of our attitudes towards ministry. I call this the "Moses Model." This model presents a distorted approach to the practice of ministry. Though disavowed in the biblical narrative, it still holds sway over our understanding, emotions and practice. In later chapters, I will review our human identity and some key principles of creative activity underlying the creation narrative in Genesis. I believe these have many implications for ministry. We will also investigate the ministry of Jesus to see how His style can contribute to the reframe we so urgently need.

Deactivating the Guilt Button

Second, reframing ministry would have *evident positive emotional consequences*. Those who serve under the prevalent understanding of ministry experience a variety of harmful emotional consequences. They often struggle with many negative emotions, including inappropriate guilt, fear, worry, anxiety and boredom. In addition, ministers often show signs of tremendous emotional exhaustion. They become emotionally spent from constantly giving themselves to others without personal retreat. Inevitably, the pileup of stress and difficulty in coping contribute to burnout. I believe a reframe allowing a place for self-care as a foundational aspect of ministry would do much to liberate ministers from these emotional consequences. For one, ministers would be less likely to view legitimate self and family care activities as a reason for guilt. Understanding self-care as ministry would largely deactivate this guilt button. This evidently happened for one pastor who took one of my ministry seminars. Understanding self-care as ministry, he said, "Thanks! The next time I go to the gym I won't feel guilty."

A former student in my pastoral care class came to the same insight. In a reflection paper, he opened with the memorable phrase from Dr. Martin Luther King: "Free at last, free at last! Thank God Almighty, I'm free at last!" He proceeded to relate how his misunderstanding of ministry had bound him in emotional knots. Specifically, he told how guilt and a sense of his inadequacy in meeting various ministry needs had kept him in shackles. In his own words: "I was smart enough to set time aside for family and rest, but I was not smart enough to handle the guilt and related stress that came from mixed priorities. I never questioned the importance of my family time or the importance of time off, but I also spent much of the time feeling guilt and stress concerning ministry needs that had been postponed, left incomplete or simply dismissed due to lack of time." Once he saw self-care as ministry and its support by biblical data, he felt freedom from this inappropriate guilt. He continued:

> Putting a scriptural underpinning to self-care has really freed me from a lot of guilt and stress. My wife commented to me yesterday about how different I have been the last couple of weeks. She talked about

how attentive I have been to her and the kids and how good that made them feel. What a great moment this was for me. In my mind, I haven't really been more attentive. *I have been free from guilt and stress and able to focus on them while I was with them. I have no doubt that translates to the family as being more attentive*[16] [italics mine].

What a testimony to the power of a ministry reframed!

Ministry in a Different Style

Third, a reframe of ministry would certainly have *implications for practice.* We would likely find a more benevolent way to practice ministry. We would move from addictive approaches and cease to justify these habits. We would give up the illusion of our divinity and our vain attempts at playing messiah. At the same time, we would learn how to take appropriate responsibility without taking on more than necessary. Instead of trying to overfunction for and enable others, we would allow parishioners room to do some things for themselves. We would move from a tendency to develop co-dependent relationships to fostering great responsibility on the part of church members. In the process, we might discover they are far more capable than we thought. We might even discover that God has endowed parishioners with spiritual gifts with which they can meaningfully contribute to the kingdom. More significantly, we would seek to minimize those practices which contribute to self-abuse. We would stop emotionally castigating ourselves for "not doing enough and not measuring up." In short, while participating in the *doing* aspects of ministry, we would not ignore the *being* aspects of ministry.

Putting out the Garbage

Earlier, I indicated that reframe acts as *a kind of filter to keep the good in and the garbage out.* This constitutes a fourth benefit. New conceptual understandings of ministry can serve to keep misconceptions out and retain essential truths. As I see it, there are currently fundamental flaws in our concept of ministry. The deepest flaw defines ministry as an other-centered activity. In turn, this fosters disregard for oneself and one's family. From this perspective, self does not really matter. Family does not matter. All that matters is serving others. This stance slowly takes its toll on the minister.

In an article, syndicated columnist Ken Garfield writes about the Rev. Paul Rademacher. After 15 years, Rev. Rademacher, who was only 47, quit ministry. According to Garfield, he fell victim to the burnout ravaging many clergy. "When the nights and weekends arrived and he wanted to devote himself to his wife, Jacquie, and their three children, he had to devote himself to leading a service or resolving a dispute in a committee meeting."[17] Eventually, the strain was too great. Rev. Rademacher gave up his church and his call to ministry and returned to carpentry. Garfield writes, "...he had grown weary of a church world that he believes emphasizes evangelism and social action, while ignoring personal spirituality."[18] Now he can come home to his family without needing to worry about committee meetings.

I do not mean to imply that ministry never involves hardship. It does. One only has to read the account of Paul's missionary journeys to get a feel for the many sufferings he experienced while doing ministry. Or one can read the account of his many hardships in 2 Corinthians 11:22-33 to get a taste of what can happen. But largely these consequences sprang from the malevolence of persons and their hatred for the preaching of the gospel. Paul did not inflict these hardships upon himself. They did not derive from his style of doing ministry. Unfortunately, I know several ministers who suffer from self-inflicted wounds.

There are many other flaws in our understanding of ministry that have been well documented. However, I will mention just one more, implied in earlier pages. This involves the belief that ministry is the private property of an exclusive group of people. Melvin Steinbron in *The Lay Driven Church* has made a good argument against this type of thinking. He argues well that all Christians are people called to ministry.[19] Once this truth is believed and practiced, it can set the church free to meet all the needs of God's people. It can also lighten the heavy burdens that pastors bear.

Getting Priorities Straight

Reframing ministry has the potential to *refocus us on our true priorities in ministry*. So many ministers spend their time like firefighters in a wildfire. They are constantly rushing all over trying to put out small fires. But unlike these heroic firefighters who rely on each other, clergy tend to work solo. They try to do single-handedly a job that is meant for a multitude. They try to be jack-of-all-trades when in reality God called them to equip the church for the work of ministry (Ephesians 4:11-16). A reframed understanding of ministry would address some of these problems. It would provide a model that serves as a guide for making judgments and deciding how one should act in ministry. In the final chapter, I will provide a model of ministry that flows from this reframe. In that chapter I will suggest ways in which this model can inform judgments, decisions and ministry action.

I agree with Bolman and Deal that the ability to reframe situations can enrich and broaden a leader's repertoire. It certainly can help us discover creative ways in which ministry can be done. Sometimes we limit our options because we are locked into the concept of one person serving many. Liberated from this limitation, we would be free to think about the endless possibilities available when all minister. This new understanding would free us to look elsewhere in the body for those persons who are particularly gifted for a particular kind of ministry.

Beyond Self-Abuse

Reframe can also provide *an antidote to self-entrapment*. This certainly has relevance to ministry. Though we are not the source of all the difficulties we experience, we can and do create some of our problems. We sometimes allow ourselves to be hemmed in by an understanding of ministry disallowing personal freedom, leisure and humanity. In so doing, we shackle ourselves in perpetual bondage to the dictates of ministry, to workaholic tendencies and vain attempts at playing God. Small wonder so many of us feel trapped, helpless and sometimes labor in quiet despair! Reframing ministry would liberate ministers to serve God freely while serving self, family and others. It would get us beyond self-abuse mistakenly done in the name of God.

1. H.B. London and Neil B. Wiseman, *Pastors at Risk* (Wheaton, IL: Victor Books, 1993), p. 54.
2. Dean R. Hoge and Jacqueline W. Wenger, *Pastors in Transition: Why Clergy Leave Local Church Ministry* (Grand Rapids, MI: Eerdmans, 2005), p. 78. The authors noted that 85% of pastors who left ministry due to conflict indicated a lack of agreement with laity about the role of the pastor as a major cause. Fifty-four percent of those who stayed noted the same problem.
3. "The Sawdust Trail," *Pillar Monthly*, November 1997, vol. 98, no. 11.
4. "1991 Survey of Pastors," Fuller Institute of Church Growth, cited in H.B. London and Neil B. Wiseman, *Pastors at Risk* (Wheaton, IL: Victor Books, 1993), p. 22.
5. Thomas Oden, *Pastoral Theology: Essentials of Ministry* (San Francisco: Harper and Row, 1983), p. 5.
6. Mike Conkle, *Designing a Needs-Based Mentoring Program for New Pastors in the Free Methodist Church of North America* (dissertation, Asbury Theological Seminary, April 2000).
7. Paul Watzlawick, John Weakland and Richard Fisch, *Change: Principles of Problem Formation and Problem Resolution* (New York: W. W. Norton and Company, 1974), p. 95.
8. Lee G. Bolman and Terrence E. Deal, *Reframing Organizations: Artistry, Choice, and Leadership* (San Francisco: Jossey-Bass, 1997), p. 12.
9. Mark Twain, *The Adventures of Tom Sawyer* (New York: Grosset and Dunlap, 1946), pp. 18-19. I am indebted to Watzlawick, Weakland and Fisch, *Change: Principles of Problem Formation and Problem Resolution*, who used this same section as an illustration of reframe.
10. Bolman and Deal, *Reframing Organizations*, p. 12.
11. Ibid., p. 5.
12. Michael Foss, "Guiding the Self-Serve Church," *Leadership* 21:4 (Fall 2000): pp. 29-31 at 30.
13. Leadership Editors, "The Business of Making Saints" (an interview with Eugene Peterson), *Leadership* 18:2 (Spring 1997): pp. 20-25 at 22.
14. Ibid.
15. See Thomas C. Oden, *Classical Pastoral Care*, Volume Two: *Ministry Through Word and Sacrament* (Grand Rapids, MI: Baker Books, 1994, paperback ed.). See chapter 1 where Oden cites a variety of early church writers who emphasized that caring for others depends on care for oneself.
16. An excerpt from a student paper, June 2000 (used with permission).
17. Ken Garfield, "Clergyman's Collar Can Grow Much Too Tight," *Lexington Herald-Leader*, November 25, 2000, sec. C11.
18. Ibid.
19. Melvin J. Steinbron, *The Lay Driven Church* (Ventura, CA: Regal, 1997).

Chapter 2

Problems in Personal and Parsonage Life

Frames that Break Us

"Ministers under stress," the headline read. Sounds like the kind of caption one expects to find in a clergy journal, not in a local newspaper. But there it was in big, bold print. Following this attention-grabbing headline, the article chronicled the growing pressures clergy face. One of the pastors interviewed sadly confessed, "We are generally workaholics, and we're great at fixing other people, but we do not have the foggiest notion of what to do for ourselves."[1] The article quoted Dr.Wayne Fehr, a specialist in clergy issues, who agreed with this confession in the following apt description: "...They share an excessive compulsive absorption in work to the neglect of their own personal needs. There's a deeply rooted, overwhelming need to please others, to take care of everybody, to avoid conflict—but at some point it becomes too hard and everything breaks down."[2]

These problems spring from a misunderstanding of ministry. Both quotations highlight a one-sided understanding of ministry giving rise to a particular behavioral style. It's one so focused on others, it squeezes out self and family. Ultimately, this style contributes to breakdown in the life of the minister, sometimes from sheer exhaustion. Much of the time, it contributes to breakdown within the pastor's family.

I call ministry framed in this manner the "Moses Model." That's because the style evident in these statements resembles that of Moses in Exodus 18. He was so absorbed in serving others that he became oblivious to his own needs. The picture painted in Exodus 18 amounts to a personal confession: God desired and Moses wrote a candid exposé of his own ministry. At first glance, the unflattering description might surprise us. It shouldn't! All across Scripture, God provides frank insights into His most beloved servants. Scripture often instructs both by good and bad examples. That's because God unceasingly desires for us the greatest good.

I choose to discuss the Moses Model because ministry framed in this manner holds powerful sway over clergy. As the first major pastoral figure in the Bible, Moses provides powerful examples of church leadership. In many respects, he is a worthy model and justly revered. For one, he was a godly man who followed God with passion, a characteristic worthy of emulation. However, his initial approach to ministry does not merit the same emulation. Yet, given the legitimate attractions to Moses, we often feel ourselves pulled toward his pastoral style. But this style has flaws. Jethro corrected those flaws in Exodus 18: 19-23. Later, we find a similar correction from God Himself (Numbers 11:16-17). However, in spite of these corrections, many blindly follow this same old approach.

In this chapter I will analyze the Moses Model and highlight some of its characteristic flaws relating to himself and his family. These flaws emerge from considering his call in Exodus 3 and 4, and his pastoral style demonstrated in Exodus 18. I reproduce an important part of the latter passage below. I have italicized some of the more critical verses.

> The next day Moses took his seat to serve as judge for the people, and they stood around him from morning till evening. When his father-in-law saw all that Moses was doing for the people, he said, *"What is this you are doing for the people? Why do you alone sit as judge, while all these people stand around you from morning till evening?"* Moses answered him, "Because the people come to me to seek God's will. Whenever they have a dispute, it is brought to me, and I decide between the parties and inform them of God's decrees and laws." Moses' father-in-law replied, *"What you are doing is not good. You and these people who come to you will only wear yourselves out. The work is too heavy for you; you cannot handle it alone.* Listen now to me and I will give you some advice, and may God be with you. *You must be the people's representative before God and bring their disputes to Him. Teach them the decrees and laws, and show them the way to live and the*

duties they are to perform. But select capable men from all the people—men who fear God, trustworthy men who hate dishonest gain—and appoint them as officials over thousands, hundreds, fifties and tens. *Have them serve as judges for the people at all times, but have them bring every difficult case to you; the simple cases they can decide themselves. That will make your load lighter, because they will share it with you. If you do this and God so commands, you will be able to stand the strain, and all these people will go home satisfied."* (Exodus 18:13-23 NIV).

What do this passage and its context reveal about Moses' ministry and its personal and family impact? Three conclusions appear to me. First, his ministry reflected some unresolved needs. Second, it violated personal boundaries. Finally, in relation to his family, Moses seemed to have ignored or neglected legitimate family obligations. I discuss these ministry flaws in the pages which follow.

Unresolved Needs in a Minister's Life
Personality and Call

True ministry always begins with God's call. The Scriptures and the testimonies of countless clergy make this clear. Nevertheless, responding to the call can precipitate personal crisis. Resistance to the call often stands at the heart of this ordeal. Thomas Oden once observed that resistance has been the hallmark of those called to ministry. For him, resistance also demonstrates the seriousness of the one called.[3] In commenting on the call, James E. Dittes states, "At least since Moses' astonished stammering at the burning bush (Exodus 3), *the encounter with the call of God has been an exhilarating and a tumultuously troublesome adventure"*[4] [italics mine].

Resistance to the call rings true for me. I first sensed God's call in my late teens. At the time, I had been converted for a little over two years. I initially experienced a call to attend Bible college in another country. This call precipitated more than a year of constant spiritual and emotional turmoil. You see, God's call conflicted with my plans to become a lawyer. I had unwaveringly harbored this dream since age six. The dream would soon become reality: I had applied for and had been accepted to law school, and I fully expected to begin my training in the fall of that year. Trekking off to some strange island to study ministry seemed like a crazy thing to do. But I could not escape the strong call tearing at my soul. I experienced great personal anguish as I wrestled with my conflicting desires. I tried the "Let's make a deal" argument with God. I placed a counterproposal on the bargaining table: "God, let me go to law school. If You do, I will complete Bible courses by correspondence." The ploy didn't work! Nothing worked to get me beyond the anguish. I finally yielded. Fear and trepidation largely inspired my surrender. Toward the end of that period of bargaining, I feared my prayers reached no farther than the ceiling; I believed God had grown tired of my resistance and efforts at compromise. Dreading the loss of God's presence, I surrendered to the call. That capitulation, though unearthed through less than pure motives, was rooted in a deep, earnest sincerity. That halting, feeble "yes" has not wavered all these years. The "yes" has merely become deeper and more informed.

Responding to the call sometimes unfolds in this manner: we respond or choose not to respond because of some need, desire or personality flaw. Jonah provides a good example of how personal issues influence our response to God's call. His prejudice against the Ninevites led him to run away from God. Finally, he answered the call and began preaching repentance in Nineveh. His preaching met with unexpected and undesired success: the people repented before God. All of his prejudices erupted to the surface. He became an angry, pouting prophet, incensed at a compassionate God. His anger and dismay at the Ninevites' salvation boiled so hot that he begged for death (Jonah 4:1-4). This biblical episode confirms that personal issues may bias or hinder response to the call.

Though his issues differed from Jonah's and my own, Moses also resisted the call.

This call rang clear in Exodus 3:10: "So now, go. I am sending you to Pharaoh to bring my people the Israelites out of Egypt" (NIV). As he struggled with God's summons, Moses inadvertently permitted us a glimpse into his personality. To say the least, he revealed himself a most reluctant prophet. Commenting on this episode, Dittes noted that Moses was startled by this intrusion into his quiet life as a shepherd and "...mistrusted, pondered, and balked saying: 'I am nobody. What can I tell them? Don't send me. I am a poor speaker. Please send someone else.'"[5] This summary captures Moses' responses well. Moses raised all sorts of issues with God: "But Moses said to God, 'Who am I, that I should go to Pharaoh and bring the Israelites out of Egypt?'" (Exodus 3:11); "Moses said to God, 'Suppose I go to the Israelites and say to them, "The God of your fathers has sent me to you," and they ask me, "What is his name?" Then what shall I tell them?'" (Exodus 3:13); "What if they do not believe me or listen to me and say, 'The Lord did not appear to you'" (Exodus 4:1); "O Lord, I have never been eloquent, neither in the past nor since you have spoken to your servant. I am slow of speech and tongue" (Exodus 4: 10).

Questions and personal put-downs masked his resistance to the call. The underlying obstinacy seemed to flow from strong feelings of inadequacy. This inadequacy, like some subterranean spring, surged to the surface to shape his answer: "I am a nobody," he pleaded. As if in a hotly contested debate, Moses rebutted all through chapters 3 and 4. God, like a skillful debater, countered each argument. In a final, futile effort, Moses confessed his lack of eloquence, all the while verbally and masterfully resisting the call.

Does this episode demonstrate legitimate humility? Commentators favor this understanding. But I suspect it runs deeper than that. His resistance likely sprang from a sense of inadequacy. That inadequacy, deeply rooted and crusted over by resistance, repelled God's every argument. He thought so little of himself that he shrank from God's invitation. Finally, God's anger burned against Moses (Exodus 4:14). Would genuine and appropriate humility justify this angry response from God? I think not! I suspect God saw inadequacy breeding resistance and slowly spawning disobedience to the call.

Like Moses, we too may shrink from God's calling because we feel inadequate. However, should we accept the call, this same inadequacy may produce an equally inadequate style of ministry. Ministry may become a performance binge intended to bolster

27

our self-esteem. Performance in ministry and ensuing successes may become means to reinforce a fragile sense of worth.

I remember one pastor who fit this profile. He was often ensnared in performance binges. Needless to say, he exhibited beginning signs of burnout. On one burnout test, he showed signs of emotional exhaustion coupled with high personal accomplishment. As I questioned the relationship between emotional exhaustion and personal accomplishment, he quickly answered, *"That's easy! I pile up the feel goods!"* Because he gained so many affirmations and "feel goods" from performing, he did increasingly more. Ultimately, this pattern led to emotional exhaustion. I have encountered similar patterns among other ministers.[6]

Moses seemed entangled in a similar web. In Exodus 3 and 4, we saw inadequacy when God called Moses. By Exodus 18, Moses was driving himself beyond his limits, judging a great multitude, case by case, from dawn to dusk, alone. The reluctant prophet had become firmly entrenched as God's sole representative to the people, but at the expense of his own well-being.

The Pendulum Principle

Persons who feel inadequate exhibit similar behavioral patterns; they seem to swing between worthlessness and grandiosity. I call this the "Pendulum Principle." I have seen this principle operate in some ministers. One pastor showed such swings in his ministry. He often experienced periods of lingering self-doubt followed by periods of grandiose scheming and activity. The first clues to its presence showed themselves when he wrote out his self-perceptions. His list contained many disclosures reflecting inadequacy, mixed with many statements projecting a grandiose view of reality. We discussed these contrasts and their relatedness at length. The Pendulum Principle operating in his life became clearly visible. Lofty views and equally lofty goals defended him against and rescued him from feelings of inadequacy. "What do you do when you feel depressed and inadequate?" I queried. He responded immediately as though he always knew the answer: *"I set myself another impossible task."* He proceeded to relate instances when he felt he could move mountains. At those times, he attempted the impossible. Failure inevitably followed. Then disappointment, sadness and depression enveloped him like a cocoon. To pull himself from this slough of despond, he set another impossible goal. Before long, this cycle, seemingly having a life of its own, commenced anew.

This sounds somewhat like Moses. Like the young man mentioned above, Moses seems to have experienced some pendulum swings. When we first met him in the prime of his manhood, he appeared a *presumptuous deliverer*. Though an unwanted messiah, he killed an Egyptian oppressor (Exodus 2:12). When we next saw him before God in Exodus 3 and 4, the pendulum had swung; he now appeared an *inadequate and reluctant redeemer*. By Exodus 18, Moses evidently had become entrenched in another extreme, trying to serve a large multitude by himself. Living out this superhuman role totally obscured his limitations of body, emotions and energy.

The intense ministry style seen in Exodus 18 may flow from other events in his life. Up to the exodus, he had experienced frustrating times in Egypt. He had a series of near successes, quickly followed by disappointment. Who knows whether the frustrating events of Egypt served to raise again the specter of inadequacy? Then success came. Who knows whether this sweet taste drove him to push past his limits? We may never know the answer to these questions. We do know, however, that many clergy exhibit insatiable needs: the need to play messiah, to gain appreciation, approval and high esteem from others. Constantly seeking to satiate these needs, they violate their boundaries. They remind me of the pastor whom I questioned about the source of his ministry stress. He candidly conceded, "My own drivenness."

Violating Personal Boundaries
Life in a "Fishbowl"

Ministry is notorious for creating boundary problems of all sorts. Much of the time, ministers and their families are afforded little privacy and space. In one stress management seminar, a female minister told the story recounted below. The story illustrates the problem of boundaries in ministry. It prominently highlights the "fishbowl" in which clergy and their families live.

A young clergy couple had come to their new pastoral appointment. The parsonage was erected next door to the church—a common boundary problem. One day while alone at home, the couple reveled in the joys of their marriage bed. Following their tryst in their sanctuary of love, the wife, still radiant with the joys of requited love, almost floated down the stairs. Suddenly, she stopped dead in her tracks. The radiance quickly drained from her now ashen face. To her horror an old male member of the church board was standing in her kitchen. Their bedroom, filled with joyous and noisy lovemaking a few minutes ago, was situated directly above the kitchen. Finding this partial stranger patrolling her kitchen, the young wife stood there on the stairs aghast and dumbfounded. Amidst the red flush of embarrassment stamped on her face, her mind raced with a thousand questions: "What is he doing in the house? How did he get in the house? How long has he been in the house?" More importantly, "How long has he been in the kitchen? How much has he heard?" Not surprisingly, this couple felt horrified and totally stripped of their privacy. Later they learned that a number of board members carried keys to the parsonage. The board made it clear that the parsonage belonged to the congregation. Love in the bedroom above the kitchen had lost its privacy forever.

This couple obviously needed a boundary to provide them privacy in the parsonage. Shortsighted congregational policy had robbed them of this most basic need. But boundaries do not simply serve to provide space and privacy. Boundaries also prevent enmeshment. Without proper boundaries, we often confuse ourselves with people or things in our world. As such, boundaries define identity and preserve distinctness. In terms of people, boundaries preserve identity by defining what is me and what is not me. In terms of things, boundaries keep us from confusing our real identity with our work identity. When we make the latter mistake, we tend to devote all of our time and energy to work. As a result, we may leave other important dimensions of ourselves underdeveloped as they are crowded out by endless activity.

Avoiding Distorted Responsibilities

Boundaries also relate to responsibilities. They define the limits of responsibility for self and others. Boundaries help us distinguish between what is our responsibility and what is not. In *Boundaries*, Townsend and Cloud emphasize the need to know one's responsibilities in the major dimensions of life. To fail to make boundaries means embracing distorted attitudes about responsibility.[7]

The relevance of this aspect of boundaries to pastoral work should readily appear. In practice, pastors sometimes demonstrate distorted responsibilities. As a result, they become overresponsible for others and the church's work. Two unfortunate problems ensue. First, those served often become underresponsible for themselves and for ministry. Second, overresponsible ministers become underresponsible for themselves and their families. Applying the concepts of overresponsibility and underresponsibility to Moses' ministry in Exodus 18 yields the following analysis:

Overresponsibility for others
1. Doing ministry from morning to evening.
2. Trying to do the entire ministry including high priority and low priority tasks.
3. Failing to engage others in the work of ministry.
4. Not setting limits on how much he would do for others.

Underresponsibility for self and family
1. Demonstrating little if any ownership of his time.
2. Ignoring his limitations of emotion and energy.
3. Neglecting proper self-care.
4. Failing to find time for his family amidst his ministry to others.

Because of distorted responsibilities, a driven, self-sacrificial approach to ministry followed. At first sight, this seems good pastoral style. It is not. Rather, it reflects enmeshment in ministry: one person trying to do everything for everyone. Such a style carries dire personal, family and congregational consequences. In

Exodus, these consequences had sufficiently budded so that
Jethro saw the future fruit. Bitter fruit awaited Moses and Israel.
Like a farmer envisioning a blighted crop, he predicted the
inevitable harvest: *"You and these people who come to you will only
wear yourselves out. The work is too heavy for you; you cannot handle
it alone."* Content with diagnosis, some might have avoided
remedy. Not Jethro! He proceeded to advocate the solution. Some
call it the "Jethro Principle." This principle "...enables more
people to share the leadership load so that God's grace works
through many and spares anyone excessive heaviness."[8]

The Forgotten Self

Not surprisingly, ignoring boundaries is costly to personal
well-being. This grave error leads to forgetting ourselves, living
outside the boundaries of time, emotion and energy, and
climbing an inhuman pedestal. We see all of these consequences
in Moses. Careful consideration of Exodus 18 shows Moses
abandoning self-care for service to Israel. This self-forgetful style
constituted a key characteristic of his style of ministry. Total
immersion in pastoral activities forms the other side of this
pattern. Moses, insensible to personal consequences, completely
engulfed himself in serving others. Apparently blind to his
absorption in ministry, he continued this harmful pattern.

Blindness to oneself and one's needs constitutes a strange but
frequent reality in ministry. Inundated by activity, clergy on the
verge of burnout usually fail to recognize their condition. Driven
activity rarely promotes self-reflection and awareness. Someone
else must illuminate the minister's darkness. Spouses or other
caring persons often become the light-bearers. In Moses' case,
Jethro alone enlightened him about his sacrificial style and its
ruinous consequences. Why didn't Aaron or Miriam say
something?

Two explanations for this lack of confrontation readily
emerge. First, Moses' status might play a part. For example,
because of his position as leader, Moses might have been
perceived as unapproachable. Therefore, though others saw his
self-injurious behaviors, none dared confront him. In the case of
Moses this is conjecture. However, lots of preachers create this
type of situation. They furiously drive themselves to greater

performance goals. Yet they exude an aura that shouts, "Don't dare approach! I stand above criticism." Though many love and care for them, few people muster courage enough to confront.

Second, the Israelites' needs may explain the lack of challenge to Moses. After all, they had a good thing going. They had a shepherd who remained perpetually available—one who appeared tireless and who loomed larger than life. He exuded perpetual divine wisdom and rendered flawless judgments. Why limit a good thing? Why rock the boat? Why remind this god-like man of his human need for rest?

Untouched by the blindness of Moses, his desert-dwelling father-in-law readily discerned the problem. Undaunted by Moses' aura, Jethro dared to question. Breaking the silent selfishness of Aaron, Miriam and the rest of the Israelites, Jethro protested. Every pastor needs a Jethro—someone who courageously cares enough to confront. Jethro challenged Moses in a chastening voice that paradoxically sought to bring healing: *"Why do you alone sit as judge, while all these people stand around you from morning till evening?"* He understood Moses' actions but not their excessiveness. He undoubtedly knew the tradition of the tribal sheik serving as judge. But he sought to highlight how Moses' extreme implementation of the tradition was hurting him and the people. Two potent images emerge from the passage. In the first image, one solitary man judges a teeming multitude of over two million. In the second image, Moses sits before expectant, weary people who stand. Both images, evoked by contrast, imply the potential exhaustion of Moses and the people. The images highlight overextension in time, emotions and energy. These problems inevitably occur when ministry is framed in a manner that excludes the well-being of the minister.

The Overextension of Time

Consider Exodus 18:13, where Moses judged the people from morning until evening. A pretty long, tiring day! One logically concludes that his schedule constituted the rule, not the exception. As in Moses' case, overcommitment in time stands as a perennial problem for clergy. In a study I conducted, time emerged as a key problem. One pastor echoed Moses' predicament. He confessed that his greatest stress derived from *"long hours—high expectations—few leaders—too many people for one man."* To emphasize my point, I have reproduced verbatim some time-related responses from this study. The responses revolve around important elements of the minister's life: self, family and parish. Failure to find or manage time in these areas stands as the heart of the problem.

"Lack of time to pursue recreation and hobbies which relax and energize me."

"Not enough time to do all that I would like both in the church and personally (fishing, relaxing, etc)."

"Time for family and self."

"Family needs, church family needs—to be in two or three places at the same time."

"Balance of job, ministry, wife time, children time, free time."

"Need for family cohesiveness, solidarity and time together vs. need to succeed at church (i.e. spend time there)."

"Lack of time with my family. Wanting to do a good job and therefore never feeling there is enough time."

"Frustration/guilt for lack of time spent with family."

"Time management, crisis management, balance between church and family time."

"Lack of time for accomplishing tasks, lack of time for family."

"Limits of time, pressures of expectations, despair and lack of motivation in the church."

"Time to get everything done."

"Too many ideas but little time to implement."[9]

These responses should surprise no one acquainted with ministry. Lack of time constitutes a key pastoral problem. The failure to manage time as a resource usually creates great havoc in the lives of ministers. These problems often hinge on overcommitment but are compounded by underestimation. That's because persons who overcommit usually underestimate the time needed to complete their commitments. The task estimated to take an hour actually requires six. The two-hour task consumes ten hours. Overcommitted ministers soon find themselves working against the clock. Hours quickly evaporate. Desperately, they borrow from the only banks left with any resources: personal time, sleep time and family time.

Exhaustion in Emotions and Energy

Moses also overexerted himself in emotion and energy. His ministry style likely drained him mentally, emotionally and physically. According to Jethro, exhaustion loomed on the horizon. Many features evident in Moses' ministry style correspond to contemporary understandings of burnout.[10] That embryonic burnout flowed directly from trying to meet all the needs around him. Like many pastors today, he apparently fell into a fatal error: assuming ministers must meet all the needs they discover around them. Such thinking, even when well-intentioned, leads to intoxicating work binges. In the article on ministers under stress quoted earlier, one pastor recounted:

> I allowed my life to become a work binge of giving, giving, giving, until I gradually became aware of my own pain and loneliness. Over time, I moved from being physically tired to emotionally exhausted and finally wiped out. I was angry at myself and angry at God—just spiritually drained. While I've never been one to talk about hell, I woke up one day and felt scorching heat all around me. I had burned out.[11]

Do-it-all preachers remind me of a church leader I knew several years ago. He often boldly proclaimed, "I would rather burn out than rust out." At that time I was in my formative years in ministry. Back then, those brash words sounded convincing, like a principle worthy of emulation. I have since grown smarter. Now this way of thinking and acting seems the height of folly. Why would God intend these extremes? Engaging others to participate in God's work seems an equally plausible intention. God desires endurance, not burnout. Endurance better accords with His love for His servants and their well-being. No wonder this goal of endurance emerged in Jethro's principle (Exodus 18:23).

I do not know exactly why Moses attempted his Herculean feat. His answer to Jethro in Exodus 18:16-17 suggests he felt driven to do it because the needs came directly to his door. The people came to him, not to anyone else. Directly confronted with these needs, he did not think he could send the people elsewhere. He did not seem to think he could involve others to help care for these needs. Ministers struggle with a different problem today. They often struggle with the "walk on water syndrome"—the belief that because one is a minister one can do anything. This appears as a common tendency in ministers. The fallacy largely derives from misframing ministry and the minister's humanity. The following statements made by members of the clergy reflect both misconceptions. The statements are actual comments from pastors attending my Stress in Ministry seminars. They all represent answers to the question, "What is a minister?" For this group, a minister is one who...

... should never get tired or fed up.
... should be available when needed.
... must always be there.
... must be everything to everyone, every time.
... should be able to do it all.
... should meet all their [the congregation's] needs.
... is never expected to be sick.
... is expected to be perfect.
... should work beyond your [sic] hours.
... should preach exciting messages every Sunday.
... should be competent in all areas of ministry.

One exhausted pastor who responded to a question about stress tiredly wrote: "The job has so many hats to wear— evangelist, teacher, pastoral counselor, custodian, administrator, preacher, home visitor, hospital visitor, moderator etc."[12]

What an unbelievable list! What do these demands and expectations suggest? As unbelievable as it sounds, the answer seems clear: ministers believe ministry demands superhuman effort and superhuman people. To do ministry one must become a demi-god. Who else but God could do all that is implied in these statements? Who else but God would even try?

Life on a Pedestal

Ministers, seemingly superhuman, ascend the pedestal. When they accept this exalted position and its stifling expectations, trouble lurks. I now emphasize in seminars: *"People on pedestals don't have needs."* Idolized preachers rise above mundane needs for self-care, recreation, sleep and regular meals. Glorified pastors seem much like the statue of John Wesley at Asbury Theological Seminary. Wesley braves driving thunderstorms, blistering summer heat, freezing cold, and the seasonal pranks of students. I have seen Wesley dressed in green on St. Patrick's' Day, wearing bunny ears and tail while carrying an Easter basket during Eastertide, and "snowman Wesley" after a heavy snowfall. Yet he remains unfazed. He stands with outstretched hand almost beckoning, appealing to the world. He has no needs. Unfortunately, too many clergy succumb to this superhuman image. Ministers wishing to express and meet their human needs must descend the pedestal. They must become real people. They must make room for real needs in their lives. They must become persons who both give *and receive* ministry.

Strangely enough, ministers sometimes struggle with having and showing human needs. We sometimes shudder at appearing human and exposing our clay feet; we falsely assume appearing mortal means losing the respect of our people. Actually, that's the furthest thing from the truth. People already know our fragile mortality. Projecting a superhuman image must make us appear as frauds. Insightful parishioners must laugh at our futile efforts to appear more than mortal. Pastors with real human needs actually appear more attractive to needy parishioners. They seem more approachable simply because they appear human like the people they serve.

I love the unfeigned manner in which Jesus lived out His humanity; He lived the human as easily as He did the divine. He seemed comfortable expressing His needs. For example, in Gethsemane, Jesus could already see the lengthening shadow of the cross (Matthew 26:31ff). His humanity, reflected in the desire to survive, inspired His anguished prayer: "My Father, if it is possible, may this cup be taken from me. Yet not as I will, but as you will" (Matthew 26:39). In stark contrast, Peter, confronted with imminent persecution because of Christ, loudly denied his need to survive (Matthew 26:33-35). Yet Peter, having so boldly disavowed his need for security and life, later denied Christ so that he might live. Because he first denied his humanity, his needs crept up on him unawares and unwittingly brought about the denial of his Lord.

But Jesus never denied His humanity. In fact, He lived out the whole wonderful range of His personhood. He celebrated weddings and other life passages (John 2:2). He attended dinner parties in His honor (Luke 7:36). He wept at the death of a friend and the anguish of relatives (John 11:35, 38). He became angered when greedy men exploited others (John 2:13-16). In his resurrection state, He even had time for a "fish fry" on the seashore (John 21:1-9). What a human! What full range of humanity! What a model! Unafraid to show His physical needs, His humanity and His clay feet! Should ministers who follow Him do less?

The Forgotten Family

Framing and doing ministry the Moses way doesn't only negatively affect the minister. It also carries serious implications for the minister's family. In a nutshell, this framing often contributes to forgetting, ignoring or neglecting one's family. Rather than an ally in ministry, the pastor might see his family as a competitor, vying for valuable time which could be spent serving others. In this battle for time and attention, the minister's family often loses. This problem seems evident in Moses.

Crowding Out Family

The length of Moses' family absence remains clouded. Exodus 18:2-4 suggests Moses had sent his spouse and children back to Midian upon his arrival in Egypt. When they finally returned, Moses provided no written account of his interaction with them. There is nothing in the passage to suggest this. However, commentators generally believe some extended and meaningful interaction occurred. They assume a joyful reunion, unreported because it marked a private family event unimportant to salvation history. Perhaps they are right. Nevertheless, given the pressing demands on Moses' time and the rapid flow of the narrative, it's easy for me to believe that little time remained for significant interaction with his family. Moses seemed focused on judging the people's disputes even on reunion day. The next day he quickly returned to his usual routine. This schedule would likewise crowd out meaningful family time. Even if I have erred in my interpretation of Moses, finding time for family is frequently a major problem for today's pastors. Many of us know clergy who find little time for their families, seeing them as distractions to *real* ministry. In pastor-spouse retreats I have conducted, clergy wives constantly raise these sorts of issues.

Ministers Missing in Action!

Pauline Boss' concept of boundary ambiguity sheds light on how absorption in work detracts from quality time with one's family. Boundary ambiguity occurs when a family does not know "who is in and who is out of the family."xiii In these cases, for a variety of reasons, a family member may be physically and/or emotionally unavailable to the system. Families caught in this uncertainty experience instability; they do not know whom to rely on to fulfill essential roles. Stability depends on adult members fulfilling roles such as providing nurture, physical and expressive needs. Absent members leave these needs unattended and so create an imbalance within the family. Generally, boundary ambiguity poses little problem if it's short-term. However, when prolonged, it creates difficulties and stress.

Pauline Boss also used the term "high boundary ambiguity" to describe families who endure long absences of members. She reported two kinds. The first type exists when a member is *physically absent but psychologically present*. The family remains emotionally preoccupied with the absent member. Examples include families with missing children, or cases involving political hostages or MIA's. The second type occurs when a member is *physically present but psychologically and emotionally absent*. The family remains intact, but a member is still unavailable. Debilitating illnesses and addictions to substances or work often lead to the latter kind of high boundary ambiguity.

Applying this concept, many clergy families experience high boundary ambiguity. Ministers often are *physical MIA's*; their long absences create major stress in their families. One former pastor illustrates this well. Prior to resigning and turning in his credentials, he led a large, growing church of 2,700 members. Moreover, the church was in the midst of a building program. As a result, the pastor put in 100-hour weeks. His weekdays started at 7 a.m., and Sundays began at 5:45 a.m. Furthermore, there were meetings on top of meetings. All these time demands left precious little time for his spouse and three children. In a desperate attempt to find time for his family, he tried to limit himself to no more than 20 consecutive nights out of the house. This same minister recalled a Sunday morning when his middle child came up to the communion rail for the children's sermon. Afterwards, she remained clinging to the communion rail because she didn't want to leave a daddy who wasn't home enough.[14] Her daddy was missing in action.

At other times, ministers become *emotional MIA's*. They are physically at home but emotionally unavailable to their families. Time at home may involve brooding over parish concerns or preoccupation with serving others. One pastor told of his obsessive fixation on Mark, a substance abuser he had befriended and brought into his home. But Mark didn't really want help and often returned to his drug habits. The pastor's need for Mark's friendship and recovery became an obsession. He was so consumed with Mark that he had little energy left for his family. He sadly confessed, *"I was a basket case at home, unable to provide emotion-ally [sic] for my family"*[15] [italics mine].

Alternately, unavailability may spring from physical and emotional exhaustion. Pastors may just be too physically and emotionally spent to give to needy family members. Both kinds of high boundary ambiguity likely applied to Moses; he remained physically absent for an extended period. From our earlier discussion, he likely now demonstrated emotional absence from his family.

Physical and emotional absence contributes to stress in clergy families. Emotionally or physically absent persons multiply pressures on their households; they cannot fulfill the roles on which family well-being hinges. Families with "missing" adults resemble alcoholic households. In such families, incapacitated alcoholics neglect many vital responsibilities like providing care, nurture and discipline. For stability, spouses or eldest children often assume the missing roles. Ministers' families experience the same problems. When clergy become workaholics, they add pressure to their homes. Workaholic tendencies deprive clergy families of a needed member, thereby adding to their stress. However, clergy do not often see workaholic behaviors in this light. Indeed, they may perceive constant involvement as the epitome of good ministry. Sometimes, a family crisis must occur to bring sobriety. Sometimes, awareness comes too late.

Ministry Is Way More Important Than Family!

Workaholic clergy send an unfortunate message: *ministry to others is way more important than family.* These ministers largely conform to John Scanzoni's *sect-type clergy.* Sect-type pastors generally ignore or neglect their families. According to Scanzoni, they exhibit the following characteristics:

1. The kin group is seen as a competitor to ministry.
2. A greater priority is given to the clergy role.
3. The ministry role stands at a higher level than the marital and family role.
4. In times of role conflict, the ministry role takes precedence.
5. Ministers are consumed with ministry to the exclusion of marital, family and expressive roles.
6. These ministers live according to a total-work orientation.[16]

Those who work with pastors can readily cite examples. I remember one pastor whom I will call "John." I would guess that

John was around 50 years old, although he appeared older. His hair was tinged with a silvery gray suggesting both distinction and the constant pressure of ministry. He was the pastor of a large, successful church. I met John during a clergy stress seminar I was leading. After the seminar, John and I talked about his ministry. During the conversation, he acknowledged a work week spanning more than 90 hours. I quickly asked how much he slept. Not surprisingly, he didn't sleep much, perhaps four to five hours per night. With a hint of regret in his voice, he confessed a great debt to his wife. She had shepherded the spiritual well-being of their children who were now fully grown. He had labored so undistracted in ministry that he had spent little time with his children. Though his behaviors did not appear deliberate and calculated, they still led to neglecting vital family roles.

Sect-type clergy remind me of the words of a popular evangelist. In one message he recounted his orientation to ministry. He revealed that in his earlier days he had little time for anything but ministry. Reading a novel amounted to the worst of sins. Of picnics and similar diversions, he asserted, "Picnic! I have no time for picnics." Yet he was married with children. I wonder if his spouse and children felt the same way about picnics. I also wonder how much time he spent consumed in ministry to the neglect of his family's needs, needs that he could partly meet through recreational activities like picnics.

Though family often seems like an intrusion to sect-type ministers, if pushed, most ministers would assert family's priority over ministry. At a minimum they would see family on par with clerical work. Nevertheless, their actions betray something quite different. As we all know, actions often speak louder than words. And clergy families are getting the message loud and clear: *ministry is way more important than family.*

A *Sally Forth* cartoon portrayed how we pay lip service to family but act in a totally different manner. In the strip, Sally sat at her dining room table working on some office project. Her important looking papers lay before her in neat stacks. Her preteen daughter, Hillary, stood before her and asked, "Doing work stuff again?" Sally replied, "Yeah, I'm pretty swamped." The conversation continued in the following vein:

Hillary: "Is it hard having to bring work home a lot?"
Sally: "Sometimes."
Hillary: "There's nothing more important than work, though."
Sally: **"Family's way more important than work"**[17] [emphasis mine].

No words appeared in the next frame, but Sally's look spoke volumes. Sally had just realized the discrepancy between her words and actions. She affirmed family's priority over work, yet her actions loudly proclaimed her work as most important. At least that was the message Hillary got! This incident appeared the norm, not an isolated work intrusion on family time. That much was clear from Hillary's question in the first frame: "Doing work stuff again?"

Sometime ago, I was traveling with two clergy friends. One was experiencing difficulty securing a return flight home. Against his will, he was forced to spend a few more days away from his family. He had earlier telephoned his spouse to convey the news. Later he admitted making several trips abroad in the previous five weeks. This was his third. Moreover, he needed to travel again in four weeks. During this time, he had spent just two weeks at home. In a voice tinged with regret, he related the sadness of his four-year-old daughter. Before this trip, she had looked at him and sadly inquired, "Are you leaving again?" Each trip evokes similar questions. The way he spoke, I believe the message is finally reaching him.

The meaning from these examples stands out rather clearly: some clergy pay lip service to spending time with their families, but the reality often appears much different. Unlike my friend and Sally, many of us never catch ourselves until a crisis erupts. In the succeeding frame from *Sally Forth*, she dropped everything, rose from her work and announced, "You know what? Who cares if this **junk** [emphasis mine] doesn't get done right this minute? Let's go shopping for that pair of pants you need. And we'll stop at Cookie Corner for a couple of chocolate chip monsters and then maybe we'll..."[18] As they got their coats to leave, a smile of contentment brightened Hillary's face. Her gloating thoughts signaled the punchline: "Mothers come preprogrammed. You just need to know which buttons to push."

Sally caught and redeemed herself in her daughter's eyes. Hillary got her needs met and spent quality time with her mother. In my opinion, Sally redeemed the situation for two reasons: First, she caught the discrepancy between lip service to family and her actual behaviors; her actions were speaking much louder than her words. Second, having compared work and her daughter's needs, the former looked like junk. Her formerly pressing business now paled into insignificance. Compared to legitimate family needs, work often appears like junk to sane and regretful persons.

The Minister's Dilemma: Ministry Is <u>Not</u> Junk

Herein lies the pastoral dilemma: ministers believe they perform the greatest service in the world. They are right! How then can they call pastoral activities "junk?" How can they legitimately set aside service to others to tend personal and family needs? They can only do this if they accurately reframe ministry. Ministry is not just serving others. *Serving self and family is also ministry.* In fact, serving oneself and one's family form part of ministry's first task. Serving others must sometimes yield to this essential aspect of the work. This kind of ministry reframe would liberate clergy to do ministry at home.

Our Lord Himself provided insight into this dynamic. In Mark chapter 6, Jesus called His disciples to rest and care for themselves. To do so, they had to leave other people's needs behind. Apparently, Jesus recognized self-care as genuine ministry that must happen even when multiple needs clamor for time and attention, demanding we neglect ourselves. In my opinion, this principle also extends to one's family. Ministry to others remains important, not junk. But serving self and family constitutes ministry *par excellence.*

Unfortunately, ministers come preprogrammed. We are programmed from a variety of sources: cultural norms extolling the virtues of achievement and doing; modeling by older ministers; constant, stifling expectations and demands from parishioners; frequent exhortations by denominational leaders; and sometimes, Bible college and seminary education. This programming frames ministry almost exclusively as acts performed for others. As a result, we often ignore a desperately needed form of service: serving self and family. So clergy families feverishly push the button. But the button does not respond. The button is exclusively programmed for providing pastoral care to others. Only persons outside the family can push the button and get a response.

Scanzoni also described *church-type clergy*. According to him, this latter group practices the following attitudes and behaviors:

1. The kin group is seen as an ally deserving support.
2. A greater priority is given to marriage and family roles.
3. Both occupational and family roles are seen as equally important.
4. In times of conflict, the family role takes precedence.
5. This approach to ministry allows for de-roling as well as fulfilling marital, family and expressive roles.
6. The approach to ministry is a work-home orientation.[19]

These characteristics show a distinctly different approach to ministry. Unlike sect-type clergy, these pastors see family ministry as a genuine obligation. Moreover, they give more than lip service to family. They see their families as allies deserving support and pastoral care. Their families respond in kind: they support the pastor's work. In contrast, sect-type clergy families often perceive ministry as an enemy. Sometimes God, who called the spouse, also becomes an enemy. I fear too many clergy treat service to others like an "affair." Their families often reciprocate with bitterness and antagonism toward God, the minister and ministry. These problems would largely be solved if ministers reframed ministry to include serving their own and their families' wellbeing.

1. Hank Whittemore, "Ministers under Stress," *Parade Magazine, Lexington Herald Leader*, April 14, 1991, p. 5.
2. Ibid.
3. Thomas Oden, *Becoming a Minister* (New York: Crossroads, 1987), p. 26.
4. James E. Dittes, "Tracking God's Call: Basic Theoretical Issues in Clergy Assessment," in *Clergy Assessment and Career Development*, eds. Richard A. Hunt, John E. Hinkle, Jr., and H. Newton Malony (Nashville: Abingdon Press, 1990), p. 21.

5. Ibid.
6. Anthony J. Headley, *Personality Characteristics on the Minnesota Multiphasic Personality Inventory and Burnout among Persons in the Ministry* (Ph.D. dissertation, University of Kentucky, 1992). Emotional exhaustion was evident in this study. On the Maslach Burnout Inventory, 78% were in the moderate and high range on Emotional Exhaustion, and a similar high number had a strong sense of Personal Accomplishment.
7. Henry Cloud and John Townsend, *Boundaries* (Grand Rapids: Zondervan, 1992).
8. Thomas Oden, *Pastoral Theology* (San Francisco: Harper and Row, 1982), p. 157.
9. Anthony J. Headley, unpublished dissertation data.
10. Herbert Freudenberger, *Burnout: The High Cost of High Achievement* (New York: Anchor Press, 1980). Freudenberger originally coined the term "burnout." It becomes particularly problematic among overcommitted and overdedicated persons. Also see Christine Maslach, *Burnout: The Cost of Caring* (Englewood Cliffs, NJ: Prentice Hall, 1982). Also see A. M. Pines, E. Aronson and D. Kafry, *Burnout: From Tedium to Personal Growth* (New York: The Free Press, 1982). The latter authors see burnout as the result of constant or repeated emotional pressure resulting from intense involvement with people over long periods of time. These marks of burnout fit the Exodus passage well.
11. Whittemore, "Ministers Under Stress," p. 4.
12. These are actual comments from ministers taken from seminars on stress in ministry.
13. Boss, Pauline, *Family Stress Management* (Newbury Park, CA: Sage Publications, 1988), p. 73. See chapter 4, pp. 72-85, for a discussion of boundary ambiguity.
14. Ken Garfield, "Minister leaves flock to tend family, self," *Charlotte Observer*, July 11, 1994, p. 1A.
15. Robert, J. Morgan, "The Need to Be Needed," *Building Your Church through Counsel and Care: 30 Strategies to Transform Your Ministry*, ed. Marshall Shelley (Minneapolis: Bethany House, 1997), p. 89.
16. John Scanzoni, "Resolution of occupational-conjugal role conflict in clergy marriages," *Journal of Marriage and Family* 27:2 (1965): pp. 396-398.
17. Greg Howard and Craig MacIntosh, *Sally Forth*, dist. by King Features Syndicate, *Lexington-Herald Leader*, February 18, 1996.
18. Ibid.
19. Scanzoni, "Resolution of occupational-conjugal role conflict in clergy marriages," pp. 396-398.

Chapter 3

How We Affect Congregations

For over a decade, Pastor Hurley served successfully as the leader of a large church in a mainline denomination. During his tenure, the church tripled in membership. Two thousand new members had joined during this time. Given this rapid growth, the church needed to expand its facilities and had initiated a $7.5 million-plus building project. Everything seemed to be going well. In the midst of this success, Pastor Hurley shocked his congregation when he announced his resignation and turned in his clergy credentials. This unexpected turn of events did not arise because of moral lapse, though it was believed to be so at the time. Rather, he indicated that his departure stemmed from the toll ministry had taken upon him and his family. After some 20 years in ministry, the pressures had become too overwhelming. His health had eroded and his family had been deeply impacted because of the stress. Hundred-hour weeks and the heavy burden of care for 2700 members robbed his wife and three children of his time and availability. So at 44 years of age, this apparently capable pastor left ministry. Neck surgery and marital stress told him it was time to go. He noted, "You don't turn in your credentials without a tremendous amount of prayer and reflection….It allows me to back away. It gives me complete time and freedom to let God walk in my life in some healing ways."[1]

This story illustrates the connection between one's ministry frame and personal, family and church fallout. As I have demonstrated earlier, an erroneous view of ministry usually leads to many negative consequences for pastors and their families. These consequences are evident in the story. But the negative impact doesn't stop there. The consequences often travel from the parsonage door to the church door. Congregations also suffer. In this case, the congregation was bowled over when the pastor announced his resignation. "Everybody from small children to older folks were crying,

47

tearfully accepting the news for the first time," said the chairman of the administrative board. "Folks are surprised and disappointed. There were those who were wondering why."² Congregations left in this state are often disappointed, perplexed and hurt. Long after the pastor has left, the emotional consequences of their unexpected demise might ripple through the congregation.

This scene isn't just a modern occurrence. The portrait of Moses' ministry in Exodus 18 and his own reactions in Numbers 11:11-15 present a similar picture. Moses' behaviors posed a potential hazard not only to him and his family, but also to the congregation of Israel. What are some of the problematic pastoral attitudes and behaviors that affect congregations? A consideration of the Exodus passages suggests the following:

1. A do-it-all approach to ministry.
2. Never saying no to burdensome demands.
3. Rationalizing one's pastoral style and thereby resisting change.
4. A ministry style that works against its best intentions and goals.

By these behaviors Moses intended to benefit Israel. Paradoxically, he was on the verge of unintentionally harming them. That's invariably the case when a pastor serves in this manner. Once a pastor and congregation become locked into this style, the idea of a nation of priests is essentially eliminated; the spiritual gifts of people in the pew become stymied. Besides this, the resulting pastoral overload invariably has repercussions for the church. To borrow from a frequent saying of Dr. Maxie Dunnam, former president of Asbury Theological Seminary: "As the pastor goes, so goes the church." Pastors and people are locked in an ongoing systemic relationship; change in one often leads to change in the other.³ Jethro evidently knew this. In two places in the Exodus passage, he clearly tied the well-being of Moses to that of the people. First, he knew that if Moses wore out, the people would wear out: "Moses' father-in-law replied, 'What you are doing is not good. *You and these people who come to you will only wear yourselves out. The work is too heavy for you; you cannot handle it alone*'" (Exodus 18:17-18 NIV, italics mine).

Second, he knew that if Moses shared the burden of ministry with others it would result in the well-being of both. For this reason, he gave the following advice:

> But select capable men from all the people—men who fear God, trustworthy men who hate dishonest gain—and appoint them as officials over thousands, hundreds, fifties and tens. Have them serve as judges for the people at all times, but have them bring every difficult case to you; the simple cases they can decide themselves. *That will make your load lighter, because they will share it with you. If you do this and God so commands, you will be able to stand the strain, and all these people will go home satisfied* (Exodus 18:21-23 NIV, italics mine).

That's always true. Pastoral health and the parishioners' well-being are inextricably linked. If the pastor does well, the benefits of that health will be felt throughout the congregation. On the other hand, if the pastor suffers, one can expect adverse consequences in the congregation. The reverse is also true. Congregational attitudes can affect the pastor. However, as leaders, pastors are critical to setting the tone within congregations. Their attitudes and styles possess great power for influencing a congregation. That's where this chapter comes in. As we investigate Moses' attitudes and behaviors identified earlier, we may learn valuable lessons on how our styles can affect congregations. In observing some of the negative impact of our styles, we may learn to frame ministry in a more beneficial manner.

Pastor Do-it-all

Moses evidently tried to do it all. That's apparently how he understood his ministry to Israel. Unfortunately many pastors are like Moses in this respect. They attempt to do many tasks within the life of the church that could easily be done by parishioners. As a result, they often find themselves overloaded and overextended. This evidently was part of the problem of the pastor we encountered at the beginning of the chapter. Several facets of overextension were evident in the article. In addition to the problems highlighted earlier, he spearheaded the construction of a $3.75 million sanctuary. He faced the challenge of planning a future $4 million classroom. For over six years he had preached three sermons each Sunday, until the church wisely cut back to two services. Furthermore, he ministered to this congregation of 2,700 members with one full-time and 2 part-time associate pastors.[4] No wonder he felt burdened enough to quit. The demands were simply too much for one person to handle well. The result is the same whenever pastors try to perform every function within the body of Christ.

Why do pastors take this approach to ministry? I suspect it's because they misinterpret ministry's meaning and mission. They forget that ministry requires clergy to equip church members for the work of ministry, not control it all. In *Pastoral Theology*, Thomas Oden remarked that "...it is pride and overweening control that causes the pastor to try to do the work of an entire congregation."[5] According to him, clergy must ensure that things get done, not unilaterally do them. This pastor evidently violated this principle. The same can be said of Moses. Exodus 18 features a man who apparently forgot other people could serve. Yet elsewhere he bemoaned how heavily the people burdened him (Numbers 11:11-14). I do not mean to criticize Moses unduly, or overstate the case. The fact is, he clearly ignored God's people as resources. He did not even seek to engage Aaron in this work. A surprising oversight since Aaron was given as his right-hand man. Surely Aaron could have shared a part of the heavy judicial load. It took a pagan priest to show him the light.

Excluding Others from Ministry

Moses' do-it-all stance excluded others from assisting him and serving each other. The same is true for ministers today. If we frame ministry exclusively as service done by clergy, this effectively excludes others from ministry involvement. Ministry framed in this manner is a one-way street running from the pastor to others. It never runs in the other direction. There's no place for the mutuality of caring which ought to characterize the body of Christ. Pastors may further exacerbate this error by pretending they never need care from others. But the same error affects the congregation. It negates the idea and practice of lay ministry.

That's the exact opposite of what God desires. God desires lay involvement in ministry. In the immediate context of Exodus 18, we catch glimpses of this divine intention. Jethro's principle involved delegating ministry responsibilities to others, shaping ordinary people for service within the kingdom. Elsewhere, in Numbers 11:16-17, Moses ascribed this delegation model to God. To lighten Moses' load, God took seventy men and placed Moses' Spirit on them. Even two others who were not part of the seventy were infused with the Spirit and prophesied. Others were coming to share in the ministry of tending God's people.

Exodus 19:6 provides additional insights into God's vision for a kingdom of priests. There God announced, "'…you will be for me a kingdom of priests and a holy nation.' These are the words you are to speak to the Israelites." God's purpose in the passage is clear: to create a kingdom of priests who proclaim God's redemptive acts to an unbelieving world. Significantly, this image of a kingdom of priests serving God's people follows a chapter that highlights one man doing all of the ministry. The contrast couldn't be more striking: a kingdom of priests versus one man serving alone. What a departure from God's design! We can never do well when we make such radical departures from God's plan—even when we serve from good intentions. Thankfully, Moses was willing to shift his ministry frame and delegate responsibility to others. Unfortunately, we are not always as willing as Moses was to involve others in the work of ministry.

Why We Fail to Delegate

Why do we sometimes find delegation so difficult? C. Peter Wagner has noted five reasons hindering clergy from delegating ministry to lay persons:

1. They believe that subordinates won't be able to handle the assignment.
2. They fear competition from subordinates.
3. They are afraid of losing recognition.
4. They are fearful their weaknesses will be exposed.
5. They feel they won't have the time to turn the work and provide the necessary training.[6]

What lies behind these flimsy rationales? In my opinion, it is superiority and inferiority that lurk in the background. Inferiority and inadequacy appear most prominently in reasons 2, 3 and 4. Wagner highlighted a truth many of us know: personal inadequacy often serves as a primary cause for monopolizing ministry. Pastors who feel inadequate sometimes fail to delegate because they fear others might do the tasks better. They may obsessively compare themselves to others and fear they do not measure up. They seem to forget that God provides a variety of persons and gifts for different functions in Christ's body. Obviously, God does not intend that clergy alone should serve His church.

Superiority also rears its ugly head in Wagner's reasons. A heightened sense of one's importance inspires reason 1; that is, people who believe themselves to be super-competent tend to view others as less capable. Additionally, they fear sullying their reputations, giving rise to reason 3. This blending of inadequacy and super-adequacy should not surprise us. Inferiority and its alter ego, superiority, often live together. A display of superiority frequently springs from an extreme need to compensate for perceived weaknesses.

One may also see additional reasons why a sense of importance contributes to doing everything: self-exalted persons will not allow others to share acts of ministry. Sometimes they veil their difficulty in delegation by suggesting common folk cannot be trusted to do ministry. On other occasions, they fail to engage others by pronouncing them incompetent. Along with these, ministers may find a thousand other ways to keep the laity from exercising their gifts for ministry. Pastors employing these flimsy excuses remind me of Roger. He refused all help with household tasks like handling the mail. Because of this failure, the mail had been backed up for seven years waiting "proper sorting!" Because he was a perfectionist, he thought that no one in his household was competent enough to meet his standards. Like Roger, perfectionist ministers frequently find themselves backed up and overloaded. Meanwhile, the body of Christ stands in the shadows, a gifted and ready resource, but unused.

I suspect framing errors contribute to the problems Wagner cites. For example, reasons 2 through 4 all possess fundamentally flawed understandings of ministry. Reason 2 frames ministry as competition. Doubtless this is true in many quarters of the church. Sometimes clergy jostle with each other and with lay people for control of ministry. But these cases represent perverted practice. Competition in ministry is the furthest thing from the biblical ideal. Biblically understood, ministry is about *collaboration*. It's about working together for one common goal—building up the kingdom of God. Reasons 3 and 4 imply ministry is about recognition and personal endeavors to save face and obscure pastoral shortcomings. In reality, ministry is never about the pastor. Ministry is about God. It's designed to bring glory to God, not attention and recognition to pastors.

Shepherd or Rancher

Pastors caught in the multiple demands of ministry need to reframe. They need to involve others in doing ministry rather than going it alone. The church growth literature suggests such a shift. Some describe a "rancher style versus a shepherd style" of ministry if one is to grow a church beyond the 200-member barrier. In this literature, a shepherd displays the following characteristics:

1. He knows the names of all the church members and families.
2. He visits each home a number of times per year.
3. He does all of the counseling.
4. He performs all official functions such as calling on the sick, baptisms, weddings and funerals.
5. He enjoys a kind of family relationship with one and all.[7]

Church growth and leadership writers agree that pastors may be able to perform these functions in churches of fewer than 200 members. However, when churches grow beyond that number, pastors cannot keep up. At this point the rancher model becomes essential. In order to successfully handle the additional load, pastors must shift their frames. They must move from a shepherd mindset to the mentality of a rancher. Unlike shepherds, ranchers do not attempt to do everything by themselves. This does not mean that the congregation lacks shepherding. Ranchers ensure that the congregation's pastoral needs are met. They simply do not seek to meet these needs alone. They share pastoral tasks with others through delegation.

I confess some reservation regarding the language of the rancher. My unease emanates from the pleasing familiarity of the shepherd motif pervading biblical imagery. However, language aside, the shepherd and rancher motifs provide some illumination regarding Moses' ministry. Moses had served as a shepherd prior to experiencing God's call to lead Israel. As a shepherd, he customarily performed all functions for the sheep. His behaviors in Exodus 18 suggest some difficulty making the shift from tending sheep to leading people. This Herculean task necessitated a change in style if Moses wanted to serve effectively. Essentially, Moses needed to break his outmoded and ineffective shepherd's frame and construct a rancher's frame for his new leadership role. Moses would have benefited significantly from the rancher model proposed by church growth writers.

What would this shift in leadership style have meant for him? First, he would not have tried to do all the judging alone. Rather, to care for Israel, he would have delegated tasks to others. He would have focused on significant areas vital to Israel's spiritual life. In the end, these changes occurred because he followed Jethro's principle. Jethro schooled Moses by providing him with poignant insights into organizational management. Jethro sounds like a stress management, organizational development and church growth consultant all rolled into one! He advised Moses to manage his stress by changing his organizational design so as to involve more people in ministry. Such a design would meet the needs and reduce pressure on both Moses and the people.

Making a shift in ministry approach can be difficult for many pastors. It involves giving up the need to be needed. It also means giving up the adulation of those who marvel at the pastor's capacity to do so much. It was no less difficult for Moses. Giving up doing it all meant some shifts for Moses: First, the move necessitated humility to receive instruction. Second, the shift demanded acknowledging the ineffectiveness of his former style. How does a pastor admit error and not lose respect? How does one share responsibility and not feel threatened by the success of another? How does one delegate and not have it detract from one's authority? A lesser person might have pondered these questions and avoided delegation. Moses did not. He apparently took the advice and implemented it. The ease with which he made the shift implied his correct priorities; he sought the well-being of others, not self-aggrandizement. Pastors with similar right motives can easily make the shift from shepherd to rancher. And, like Moses, their reputations rarely suffer. In the process, they enhance ministry within their congregations.

Difficulty Saying No

Apparently, Moses made a second mistake. He was constantly available. Evidently, he did not say no very often. Many pastors operate in similar fashion. Because of this failure, they often do not set boundaries around their time and activities. Many wrongly believe that they must say yes to every demand that parishioners make. As a result, they rarely decline the constant demands that confront them. Blackmon and Hart call these clergy "under-assertive (passive) ministers." They describe them in the following manner:

> Under-assertive (passive) ministers are characterized by a number of factors. They generally find it difficult to set limits, they cannot say no to requests; they are easily manipulated by stronger individuals; and they are unable to express any angry feelings constructively. This often builds up to an aggressive expression of angry feelings, which leaves the minister with feelings of guilt for having made emotional outbursts. In addition, under-assertive ministers usually avoid conflict situations, and they are excessively apologetic with people.[8]

Clearly, such unassertive behaviors will affect the minister and others. Because of a failure to deal with pent-up anger, the minister may allow those feelings to build to a boiling point and subsequently explode on innocent parishioners. Much of the time these angry outbursts are directed at the very persons with whom the pastor had formerly been unassertive. Sometimes the explosion comes from innocuous incidents not meriting such a display. One can also see potentially negative congregational impact proceeding from the avoidance of conflict situations. Much of the time, potential conflict issues are not addressed until a full-scale "war" breaks out in the congregation.

Because of the potential personal and congregational consequences, it should be fairly obvious that ministers need to learn how to say no. However, this capability demands at least two ingredients: a measure of self-awareness of our limits, and sufficient assertiveness to resist the demands others make. Ministers may suffer on both counts. First, because of the god illusion, we may not always be aware of our human limitations. Our busyness doesn't help either. Busyness often serves to dull awareness of our limitations in energy and capability. Second, many pastors struggle with demonstrating assertive behavior, wrongly believing that such practices are unchristian. For these reasons, an understanding of and training in assertiveness may well prove vital to clergy's well-being.

Assertiveness involves the capacity to claim one's rights without getting angry. Ministers often need to know that they have rights, even though they may choose to sacrifice them for godly reasons. The sacrifice is only meaningful if the minister has already experienced the capacity to claim those rights.[9] Making sacrifice without having the freedom to claim one's rights or make the choice to give them up isn't Christian. It's base, slavish behavior. Many ministers live in the dark when it comes to such an understanding of assertiveness. Having little experience with claiming their rights, they may be unaware that this is sometimes a godly responsibility. As a result, they become easy prey to every whim and fancy that comes along. Furthermore, for many pastors, assertiveness may not be a matter of *choosing* to sacrifice one's rights. Instead, it often means *forced* sacrifice. Sadly, some believe that forced sacrifice is the duty to which Christ calls them. Nothing could be further from the truth! Such forced sacrifice often involves "passive weakness bordering on cowardice."[10]

But unassertive pastors are not the only problem. Sometimes ministers can go to the other extreme and become overly aggressive. If unassertive ministers find it difficult to *say* no, aggressive ministers find it equally difficult to *hear*. Given this style, they tend to ignore others' boundaries and dominate them aggressively or manipulatively.xi One pastor I read about demonstrated this style. He confessed that his leadership style involved harassing people to do things so the church could grow. Not surprisingly, there was a lot of disunity in the church. The church experienced constant fluctuations in church attendance as people came but quickly left. His style helped create many of these problems.[12] Others, disdaining the iron glove approach, may choose the velvet glove of manipulation. The outcome is the same even if the means are different. Machiavellian-like, the goal is to control and dominate those with whom they interact.

Both unassertive and overassertive behaviors generate serious consequences in ministry. Unassertive pastors may become overloaded. Overload obviously became a consequence for Moses. But that's not all. Both underassertive and excessively overassertive ministers may experience difficulties with depression, burnout and helplessness. Additionally, anger and resentment also pose difficulties for them.[13] In a study I conducted, one pastor suggested a similar cycle. He indicated his stress was connected to "[u]nrealistic self-imposed expectations (leading to) guilt (leading to) anger (leading to) sadness (leading to) depression."[14] Laboring under unrealistic expectations and failing to employ God's people frequently leads to these problems. The results remain the same whether those expectations are self-imposed or imposed by others.

But these behaviors also affect parishioners. Unassertively saying yes to all congregational demands for care may lead parishioners to become dependent on the pastor. Conditioned in this manner, they keep coming because they now believe their needs can only be met through clergy. This certainly is plausible in the case of Moses. It's not difficult to imagine how his constant availability to Israel created dependency on "the answer man" and kept them coming back. It seems the whole of Israel, Moses included, fell under the illusion of believing one man could actually serve such a multitude.

The same vicious ministry cycle happens among today's ministers. We are often guilty of failing to say no to many demands in ministry. We leave the impression we can constantly be available to every parishioner. As a result, the people keep coming, even with simple needs they could meet by themselves.

They have become dependent on clergy to satisfy their needs. Until we shift frames, they will keep coming and become enmeshed with us in an unhealthy co-dependent relationship. Remember the illustration in chapter 1? In one church, 9,500 members became dependent on a senior pastor and four associate pastors. They never changed until the pastors changed their ministry frame and equipped them to serve each other.

Aggressive ministers also affect congregations. They tend to intimidate those with whom they work. They demoralize others and thereby inspire little, if any, confidence in others. At the same time, they may build rigid boundaries, distancing themselves from church members.[15] Not surprisingly, this style fails to contribute to morale building among church staff or parishioners. Aggressive ministers who cannot hear "no" can produce more sinister consequences for others. I believe the recent increase in boundary violations and sexual misconduct stems partly from this source. Sexual misconduct usual begins with minor boundary intrusions into a parishioner's life. Eventually, these minor violations can lead to full-blown sexual contact. Significantly, these violations are much more likely to occur when a minister is overloaded and stressed. "Carnaling out"—engaging in fleshly activities—may be a perverted effort to cope with ministry demands. Even unassertive ministers who become overextended and stressed can succumb to this habit. From this perspective, unassertiveness or aggressiveness plus stress is a deadly combination which can ravage a pastor's integrity and violate a congregation.

Staying in the Same Frame

Sometimes rather than changing our ministry frame, we seek to justify our style. That seems to be the case with Moses. In Exodus 18:15-16, Moses appeared to rationalize his exhausting focus on serving others. He announced a God-given mandate to support his style. His rationale was, in his words, "...[b]ecause the people come to me to seek God's will. Whenever they have a dispute, it is brought to me, and I decide between the parties and inform them of God's decrees and laws." What an answer! What a motive! Can you see the hidden divine imperative? How does one counter this defense? In essence, Moses justified his habits by declaring himself God's answer to the people's needs. He was doing God's work. Such a glorious goal justified even inglorious means. Moses almost implied that his style and behaviors flowed directly from God's mandate.

Have you also noticed the certain conviction in his rationale? He sounds remarkably positive, not tentative or unsure. Such convictions are generally commendable. Yet, though he clearly defined his ministry, he did so to justify his behaviors. Apparently, a clearly defined ministry covers all kinds of neglect. Multiple needs in a congregation excuse working around the clock, neglecting family and slowly wearing out. Many modern day clergy delude themselves in the same fashion.

Love That Corrects

Thank God for in-laws! Strange words if one believes the all-too-frequent in-law jokes. But once we consider that Moses was slowly wearing out, we must say, as he probably did several times after, "Thank God for in-laws like Jethro!" Jethro cared enough to confront Moses. He remained undaunted by Moses' status and position. He would have none of Moses' excuses and valiant self-sacrifice. Undaunted by Moses' God-talk, he clearly confronted and corrected him: "What you are doing is not good. You and these people who come to you will only wear yourselves out. The work is too heavy for you; you cannot handle it alone" (Exodus 18:17-18 NIV). Thank God for people who love enough and are bold enough to correct our folly. Without them and their words of reproof, we would perish long before our time.

Though Jethro firmly censured Moses, he did not intend to hinder this great leader's response to Israel's needs. He did not oppose Moses serving Israel. Rather, he disapproved of Moses' method because this style ensured exhaustion from overload. If Jethro spoke today, he would likely assess potential burnout in both Moses and Israel. Many features in the passage correspond to contemporary definitions of burnout. According to these definitions, burnout stems from constant exposure to emotional pressures. Usually, persons who burn out have been intensely involved with others over long periods of time.[16] According to Herbert Freudenberger, who coined the term "burnout," certain types of people are especially susceptible: those who are idealistic and devoted to a cause, and dedicated, highly committed people.[17] Freudenberger and North recently noted other characteristics of the burnout cycle. The cycle usually begins with a compulsion to prove oneself. It continues with features such as working harder, neglecting one's needs, denying emerging problems, withdrawal and depression as one moves through the cycle toward full-blown burnout.[18] Moses' attitudes and behaviors fit well with several of these burnout characteristics and stages.

Hurting Those We Mean to Heal

One could easily miss a critical point Jethro made. He did not only envision Moses wearing out. The people would also wear out. Given his overextension, a worn out Moses makes sense. Ostensibly, the wearing out of the people makes less sense. But Jethro spoke accurately. The people would wear out. Multiple explanations for this readily appear. First, the people could become exhausted from long periods spent waiting for justice. Since Moses worked alone, his people's court would have long lines of those seeking justice. Besides this, the text pictures the people standing as they waited. There were no comfortable, cushy seats for these plaintiffs, just long lines and disgruntled people. If you have ever spent time standing in a line at a checkout counter or a government office, you know what that feels like. Sometimes it seems like an eternity before you ever get to the front of the line.

Second, some could forsake the judicial process and attempt to handle things on their own. Tired of waiting, they could decide to take matters into their own hands and seek their own brand of justice. In such cases, trouble could erupt in Israel.

Third, a worn out and stressed Moses would be more likely to dispense justice wrongly. When people are tired, exhausted and stressed, they do not necessarily think clearly. That's because stressed people sometimes experience *emotional hijack*. Emotional hijack disengages one's ability to reason and think clearly. In *Emotional Intelligence*, Daniel Goleman states: "When emotionally upset, people cannot remember, attend, learn, or make decisions clearly. As one management consultant put it, 'Stress makes people stupid.'"[19] Men and women of God are not immune from stupidity generated by stressed lives. Being called by God does not exempt us from the lapses and errors in judgment springing from being emotionally upset and exhausted. To be at our best we have to be rested and on our toes. Had he been well rested, Moses might have judged more effectively. But there is little in the text suggesting he took sufficient recesses to stay sharp. Given these circumstances, it's not difficult to imagine mishandled cases. Mishandled justice could then lead to social disruptions.

Finally, exhausted by continual demands, Moses could develop a callous attitude toward the people; the same people he now served so unselfishly. His complaint in Numbers 11:11-15, quoted earlier, may reflect his growing frustrations and negative attitudes toward Israel. In that passage, one readily sees the following indicators of his frustration:

1. The people became a heavy burden upon him (vv. 11, 14).
2. He disowned the people (v. 12).
3. He became frustrated with meeting their needs (vv. 12 -13).
4. Their continued complaints wearied him (v. 13).
5. Moses became frustrated to the point of surrendering any responsibility for Israel (v. 14).
6. He considered death preferable to continued service (v. 15).

In the current burnout literature, callous attitudes in the caregiver constitute depersonalization. Perhaps Jethro envisioned a similar process contributing to the people wearing out. The context ties Moses' exhaustion to Israel's well-being. For good or for ill, Moses' style affected Israel. That's always the case in the church—as the pastor goes, so goes the church. The slogan, *"Worn out people wear out people,"* summarizes my point succinctly. By exhausting himself, Moses was sure to eventually wear the people out. To quote a line from a *Doonesbury* cartoon, "Highly stressed, chronically fatigued employees cannot give their best." Sometimes the ones to suffer most are those served by highly stressed, chronically fatigued pastors.

What happens when pastors become stressed to the point of burning out? One of two things usually occurs. On the one hand, the burned out minister might stay and become "dead wood"—doing just enough to get by; the minister continues to serve but is clearly devoid of passion or fire. Unfortunately, many ministers choose this stance and their congregations pay the price for their lack of passion. On the other hand, many burned out ministers leave ministry altogether. This was the case with the pastor highlighted at the beginning of this chapter. We see a similar situation in Moses' ministry. Moses seemed on the verge of a similar demise and retreat from ministry. That's apparently the case in Numbers 11:11-15. He simply did too much. But Moses was not the only loser: Israel teetered on the brink of losing a capable leader who became overburdened by ministry. That's part of the irony of burnout. Burnout seems to afflict most acutely those who are idealistic, motivated and highly committed. When they burn out and leave ministry, the church often loses the service of highly capable and committed servants of God. Because of misinformed approaches to ministry, congregations are losing some of the brightest and the best.

Working Against Our Best Intentions

Before proceeding, I wish to emphasize Moses' good goals and intentions for serving Israel. He sought their greatest good by bringing God's word to bear on their lives. He sought their intimate relationship with God. This task constitutes the fundamental business of ministry. As Eugene Peterson notes: "The most important thing a pastor does is to stand in the pulpit every Sunday and say, 'Let us worship God.'"[20] Like Moses, we must work to make God real in people's lives, both in their inward life, their outward walk and daily hassles. By seeking this goal, Moses succeeded to a degree. One cannot argue with his ultimate goal. One can only question the methods which undermined his otherwise legitimate goals.

Modeling in Ministry

So, in spite of his legitimate intentions and desires, Moses' ministry habits worked against Israel's good. His style had the potential to exhaust Israel, not enhance their well-being. Additionally, his style would serve as a bad model for Israel to follow. Besides equipping ministers, modeling for those in the pew forms a fundamental task of ministry. Pastors should model appropriate behavior for parishioners to follow. Like the Apostle Paul, we should live so as to say, "Follow me as I follow Christ." Clergy who attempt to do all of the ministry negate this example. By their actions, they proclaim a workaholic style that sends the wrong message to harried parishioners. In this critical area, Moses failed to be an appropriate model.

When I speak in this manner, I know I stand guilty of judging Moses according to modern standards. But I believe the point bears mentioning. Moses modeled overwork and overextension as legitimate styles. He demonstrated that worthy goals justified self-exhaustion and self-neglect. Up to this point, modeling overextension and overwork may not have created problems in Israel. But from Jethro's perspective, complications loomed ahead. Bad modeling by clergy almost always creates difficulties for pastors and parishioners. Jethro knew that. Modern clergy often learn this lesson the hard way, after they have already become stressed out and burned out.

Stress remains one of the great problems of modern life. Nowhere does this appear more evident than in work life. Work pressures have been well documented for their deleterious impact on individuals. But stress and strain can impact many other facets of one's life. Sometime ago, a local newspaper article caught my attention. In it, syndicated columnist John Rosemond described a phenomenon he called "Frantic Family Syndrome." He referred to the hectic family lifestyle that results from racing children to various after-school activities. Normally this leads to overscheduled and overstressed parents and children. Having raised three sons, I understand how easily this can happen.

What does this have to do with modeling and ministry? Simply this. Many parishioners endure a great deal of stress that leaves them drained—pressures from the job, family pressures like the "Frantic Family Syndrome," life cycle transitions and societal changes. Pastors ought to model a different way of life that takes stewardship of self, time and other resources seriously. The last thing parishioners need is a stressed-out minister. But in the case of workaholic ministers, that's exactly what they see and get; they observe pastors whose life largely betrays the same predicament. Robert Schnase put it well when he asserted:

The last thing our high-strung, workaholic, career-driven suburbanites need is a high-strung, workaholic, career-driven pastor. Families suffocating under the anxieties brought on by their materialistic drive for success do not need their compulsive behavior applauded by their spiritual leaders.[21]

Well said! Chronically stressed parishioners find it difficult to take workaholic pastors seriously when they preach about balanced living. They must appear hypocritical since they carry beams in their own eyes while seeking to cure parishioners' specks. In a real sense, ministers working from the Moses Model lose the right to be heard. On the other hand, clergy who practice stewardship of their lives can best speak to today's stressed-out people.

---

1. Kenneth Garfield, "Minister leaves flock to tend self and family," *Charlotte Observer*, July 12, 1994, p. 1A.
2. Ibid.
3. See Anthony J. Headley, "A Systems and Developmental Perspective on the Seasons of Pastoral Life and Ministry" (unpublished article prepared for the PSALM Initiative at Asbury Theological Seminary), p. 2. This systems perspective is endorsed in several authors. For example, see C. Darling, C, E. Hill, and E. and L. McWey, "Understanding stress and quality of life for clergy and clergy spouses," *Stress and Health* 20 (2004): pp. 261-277. See also Cameron Lee, "Specifying intrusive demands and their outcomes in congregational ministry: a report on the Ministry Demands Inventory," *Journal for the Scientific Study of Religion* 38 (1999): pp. 477-489.
4. Garfield, "Minister leaves flock to tend self and family," p. 1A.
5. Thomas Oden, *Pastoral Theology* (San Francisco: Harper and Row, 1982), p. 156.
6. C. Peter Wagner, *Leading Your Church to Growth* (Ventura, CA: Regal Books, 1984), pp. 57-58. Wagner listed these reasons for ministers not delegating. He ascribed them to Ted W. Engstrom's, *The Making of a Christian Leader* (Grand Rapids, MI: Zondervan, 1976).

7. Ibid., pp. 57-59.
8. Richard A. Blackmon and Archibald D. Hart, "Personal Growth for Clergy," *Clergy Assessment and Career Development*, eds. Richard A. Hunt, John E. Hinkle, Jr. and H. Newton Malony (Nashville: Abingdon Press, 1990), p. 41.
9. Ibid.
10. Ibid.
11. Ibid.
12. Steve Mathewson, Casey Carey and Dee Duke, "Faces of Change: Three Stories of Pastors Who Grew through Transition," *Leadership* 18:1 (Winter 1997): p. 60.
13. Blackmon and Hart, "Personal Growth for Clergy," p. 41
14. Unpublished data from the dissertation study by the author.
15. Blackmon and Hart, "Personal Growth for Clergy," p. 41.
16. A.M. Pines, E. Aronson and D. Kafry, *Burnout: From Tedium to Personal Growth* (New York: The Free Press, 1982).
17. Herbert Freudenberger, *The High Cost of High Achievement* (New York: Anchor Press, 1980).
18. Herbert Freudenburger and Gail North, "The Burnout Cycle," *Scientific American Mind* 17:3 (2006): p. 31.
19. Daniel Goleman, *Emotional Intelligence* (New York: Bantam Books, 1995), p. 148.
20. Leadership Editors, "The Business of Making Saints: An Interview with Eugene Peterson," *Leadership* 18:2 (Spring 1997): p. 22.
21. Robert Schnase, *Ambition in Ministry: Our Spiritual Struggle with Success, Achievement and Competition* (Nashville: Abingdon Press, 1993), p. 73.

Chapter 4

Spiritual Consequences of the Moses Model

Paying the Price for Playing God

"Moses is the center of everything, not God!" So said a doctor of ministry student during a class on clergy burnout. I had just asked the class to read and share their insights on Exodus 18:13-23. To prove his assertion, he pointed to the dominance of the first person pronouns in the narrative. To him, Moses dominated the narrative. It seemed the ministry's success largely rested on his shoulders, not God's. Just about everyone in the class agreed with his observation and volunteered supporting evidence. They acknowledged his intent to focus the people on God, but believed he missed the mark.

The same result is possible for today's ministers. Unless we exert great care as messengers, we can easily overshadow the Giver of the message. We can inadvertently divert attention to ourselves, overshadowing God and usurping the place which rightfully belongs to Him. Moreover, seduced by workaholic drivenness and the church's acclaim, we can forget the ultimate source for ministry empowerment. We can come to depend largely on our abilities, talents and strengths to make things happen. Often this shift is not intentional, deliberate or conscious. Rather, it usually springs from zeal gone awry.

Such unfortunate consequences occur when we minister from the Moses Model. Desiring to serve and glorify God, we paradoxically draw attention away from Him as though we ourselves are God. Not surprisingly, living this divine illusion precipitates exhaustion which in turn foreshadows disaster. No human person, no matter how spiritual, can continue to work around the clock and not wear out. Unfortunately, we usually realize our fragile humanity and dire need for God when the pressures mount and we find it difficult to cope on our own. By then much of the damage is done. We have pushed ourselves so far that it's hard to circumvent the physical, emotional and spiritual consequences. We slowly begin to unravel from the inside. Eventually the consequences of this inner upheaval become public. Angry outbursts and biting remarks to others signal all is not well. We may even display resentful and angry attitudes towards God, holding Him responsible for our troubles. Before our spiritual and emotional meltdown, people considered us superhuman and spiritual giants who could never fall. Now our frail humanity and spiritual struggles are only too painfully obvious. Some of these dynamics apply to Moses as demonstrated in Numbers 11:11-15, quoted below:

> He asked the LORD, "Why have you brought this trouble on your servant? What have I done to displease you that you put the burden of all these people on me? Did I conceive all these people? Did I give them birth? Why do you tell me to carry them in my arms, as a nurse carries an infant, to the land you promised on oath to their forefathers? Where can I get meat for all these people? They keep wailing to me, 'Give us meat to eat!' I cannot carry all these people by myself; the burden is too heavy for me. If this is how you are going to treat me, put me to death right now—if I have found favor in your eyes—and do not let me face my own ruin" (NIV).

How does a spiritual giant and devoted servant of God get to ranting and blaming God for his difficulties? It didn't happen overnight. Rather, the combination of too much time in ministry, too little attention to self-care, wrong beliefs, and overextension piled up to produce these visible signs of his unraveling. This should not surprise us. Overtaxing human capacities almost always has a disastrous impact on the whole person. Sometimes it reverberates through our spiritual lives, promoting all kinds of confusion and questions about God. The unraveling we see in Moses provides a good illustration of these dynamics.

The unraveling clearly derived from behaviors associated with the way he framed ministry. As suggested in the first chapter, frames involve perceptions shaping emotions and behaviors. Each of these dimensions appears in this passage.

Moses' words reveal a misunderstanding of God and his call. We can also infer a behavioral style which gave rise to his exhaustion. In turn, these problems contributed to his negative emotional state. Painful and pent-up emotions now poured forth in unrelenting torrents cascading down on God. His emotional responses were so pronounced and his thinking so fevered they capture our attention. But each of these dimensions—the cognitive, behavioral and emotional—were deeply rooted and connected to God and spiritual realities. Cognitively, Moses now entertained different *beliefs about God and his call*. Behaviorally, he now he indulged in *faultfinding behavior directed at God and desires to give up the call*. Emotionally, *his anger and frustrations were feelings directed against God*. Each of these spiritual ramifications related to thinking, emotions and behavior merits some discussion.

Spiritual Consequences of Wrong Thinking
Misinterpreting Our Call

Sometimes wrong thinking about spiritual matters leads ministers to exhaustion. The reverse is also true. Exhausting ourselves in ministry can lead ministers to radically reshape their beliefs about spiritual matters including how they understand and respond to their call. Most of the time the two work in combination, mutually affecting each other. I suspect this was the case with Moses. Moses evidently misinterpreted ministry. From his behaviors in Exodus 18 and his language in Numbers 11, he evidently interpreted his call to mean meeting all of Israel's needs single-handedly. He saw God placing the burden of the people upon his shoulders alone, making for an all-consuming pastoral role designed to meet Israel's needs. He had to cater to their need for spiritual guidance, conflict resolution and physical nurture, and he had to do it alone. What responsibility! No wonder the load proved so burdensome he now desired to give up the call.

Moses' misinterpretation of his call reminds me of a similar error made by Boyd Larson, a first-term missionary to Liberia. Like Moses, his zeal for God led him to interpret the call in Herculean terms: "I had four years to win Africa for Jesus…and I was going to do it alone,"[1] he recalled. Imagine that! Four years to win the teeming millions of Africa by himself! Which human would possibly think God's call necessitated one person to do such a task alone? Boyd Larsen did. In the process he afflicted great pain and hardship upon himself. Physical symptoms like vomiting, diarrhea, headaches and dehydration ravaged his body. Four times in thirteen months he had to be hospitalized and hooked up to an intravenous drip. He became confused and afraid. Ultimately, his missionary board gave him 48 hours to pack and leave Africa. Only on the flight home did he confront the burnout which had engulfed him. Paradoxically, instead of helping to fulfill his dream for Africa, his zeal precipitated burnout and hastened the early demise of his ministry. Unfortunately, this is not an isolated story. Since the time of Moses, zealous servants of God have worn themselves out and prematurely cut short their ministry when God intended many more fruitful years.

Shifting Beliefs about God

Moses' misinterpretation of his call contributed to personal exhaustion. This was painfully evident earlier, in Exodus 18. But, in Exodus, we never saw the skewed beliefs now displayed towards God. Worn out and emotionally exhausted, Moses could no longer see spiritual reality clearly. He now misunderstood the nature and character of God. Instead of seeing God as trustworthy and benevolent, Moses now saw Him as One who deals falsely and harmfully with His devoted servants. God seemed angry and uncaring, rather than gracious and caring. These shifts in his view of God wreaked havoc with his spiritual sensibilities. Spiritually, he had fallen rather far. This man who once stood in the presence of God and conversed with Him face to face now accused God of heinous behavior. He accused God of afflicting him, being ungracious and unjustly placing heavy burdens on him. He berated God for his condition. Matthew Henry noted: "...Moses expressed himself otherwise than became him. He undervalued the honor God had put upon him. He magnified his own performances, while he had the Divine wisdom to direct him, and Almighty power to dispense rewards and punishments. He speaks distrustfully of the Divine grace. Had the work been much less he could not have gone through it in his own strength; but had it been much greater, through God strengthening him, he might have done it."[2]

This shift towards God seems shocking, but it is not surprising. Individuals who experience trauma and stress-related disorders often experience disruptions of personally held frames of reference. For example, persons may question their identity and capabilities. They may come to doubt previously held worldviews, including views about God and spiritual things. These disruptions often contribute to and are reflected in spiritual impoverishment. Over time this condition might show itself in "…the loss of meaning for one's life, a loss of hope and idealism, a loss of connection with others, and a devaluing of awareness of one's experience."[3] Similar problems also occur when individuals become exhausted and burned out.[4] Many of the problems identified apply to Moses. He questioned his identity and capabilities; he had lost and seemed to despise his connection to the Israelites. Most significantly, he had experienced radical shifts in his view of God.

Bad Theology Makes for Flawed Ministry

One cannot hold such beliefs and not be affected. Thinking almost always influences us in multiple ways. Right thinking usually has a positive impact. Wrong thinking—*stinking thinking*—almost always affects us negatively. The word "alone," which occurs in both Exodus 18 and Numbers 11, provides an example of wrong thinking and its effects. In the first passage, Moses wrongly believed doing ministry was a one-man show. This belief contributed to the exhausting style whose bitter fruit shows itself in Numbers 11. Ironically, serving Israel alone almost appeared as a badge of honor in the Exodus passage. But how times had changed! In Numbers 11, serving alone became the key source of his pain and anguish. That's the way it often is. The way we think about God and interpret our call gets translated into overt behaviors. If we interpret our call in terms of doing things by ourselves, that's what we will do. If we interpret our call as serving all the people and all their needs, we will try to meet these multi-faceted needs by ourselves. Our theology of God and ministry will always influence how we practice ministry. Bad theology in these areas largely contributes to workaholic tendencies that fracture us. Bad theology almost always makes for bad ministry.

Bad theology also makes us blame the wrong people once we experience failure. No wonder Moses blamed God! His blaming does not surprise me at all. Blaming and faultfinding commonly occur when one is stressed or burned out. This kind of behavior has been documented in people serving in the helping professions. Typically, those who burn out start with self-blame. As failure continues, they resort to blaming others and eventually move to blaming the systems of which they are a part. These efforts in shifting blame help them avoid responsibility. In turn, avoiding responsibility provides a faint hope of lessening their pain for not measuring up to their goals.[5]

Those of us who work with stressed and burned out ministers can attest to similar dynamics. Sometimes we encounter a great deal of self-blame. But we can also attest to a great deal of blame and bad feelings directed towards parishioners, church boards and other people within the life of the church whom pastors hold responsible for their difficulties. Over time these ministers come to blame the "system." They come to cast a great deal of criticism at denominational leaders and the bureaucracy within which they serve.[6] Moreover, even though they may not often make their blaming of God public, in private they often direct blame and vehemence toward God. These dynamics apply to Moses. We see traces of his dissatisfaction with his failure to successfully serve Israel. More evident is a lingering distaste for the people, reflecting some blame cast in their direction. But most visible is his blaming God. He pointed his finger at God and blamed Him for his woeful condition as though God had caused it. In reality, it was his own thinking about God and his call that brought the devastation. Nevertheless, having experienced the negative consequences of his beliefs and his actions, he now held God responsible. Just as burned out individuals finally come to blame the system, Moses blamed God who represented, for him, the ultimate cause of all his difficulties.

Negative Emotions in Ministry

Because he blamed God, many negative emotions in Numbers 11 were directed at Him. We see a great deal of misdirected anger. Moses displayed anger at God for his condition, even though it was his own fault. Isn't it amazing? We mess up and then blame God for our troubles. That's not surprising. Behind blame, one will often find boiling anger for some hurt, real or imagined. Sometimes we lash out at others because we cannot accept full responsibility for our own behavior which brought the devastation. We seek to dilute it by pointing our fingers at others, even God. In fact, God often bears the brunt of our attack.

I have seen the same anger in ministers I have counseled. Not everyone breaks out in overt displays of anger as Moses did. Nevertheless, I have found deep-seated anger in some pastors. Usually, ministers initially resist admitting or accepting their deep anger towards God. However, once owned, the anger often erupts like a raging volcano spewing frequent gushing torrents— all directed at God. Sometimes the anger spills over on anyone who represents God. Like Moses, pastors caught in the grip of anger often accuse God of abandonment, neglect and unjust behavior. By their words they suggest their troubles spring from God. After all, He is the One who called them into ministry.

Besides anger, other signs of emotional upheaval appear in the text. Moses spoke of his affliction, his burdensome condition and his wretchedness. To him, they all derived from the heavy burden God had callously placed upon his shoulders. Moses implicitly accused God of gross injustice. The combination of his afflicted condition, the sense of injustice and God's callous lack of care now fostered a depression so deep, Moses coveted death over life. Many of these emotional characteristics and others noted earlier suggest that Moses was deeply locked in the condition we now call burnout, or, at the very least, something that looks an awful lot like it.

According to Christine Maslach, burnout is a composite of *emotional exhaustion, depersonalization and personal accomplishment.*[7] Emotional exhaustion refers to being emotionally spent. Many characteristics already mentioned suggest such emotional overextension in Moses. This great man of God had been brought to the brink of disaster because of emotional overload. There's a message here for all of us who minister. We should never underestimate the impact of emotional overload. Exhausting ourselves emotionally can contribute to spiritual and overall turmoil in the life of the most faithful servant of God. In fact, it's not just emotional exhaustion. Exhausting ourselves in any way, emotionally or physically, can fracture us deeply and bring us to the precipice of total despair, which eventually devastates our spiritual being. Yet, in spite of the devastation exhaustion works, too many ministers ignore their need for rest and restoration. Instead, they plunge themselves into endless activity which engulfs them in exhaustion and eventually leads to the kind of unraveling evident in the text.

Signs of depersonalization also appear in Numbers. Depersonalization refers to the development of callous and uncaring attitudes toward those whom we serve. It's quite evident Moses' attitudes toward the people had shifted. He now showed impersonal and uncaring attitudes toward the people of Israel. The people had become a burden to him. His words suggest he was only too ready to be rid of them and the pressures they caused him. The third component, personal accomplishment, refers to one's sense of accomplishment and achievement in one's work. This involves having a sense of meaning derived from one's work. It seems fairly obvious that Moses had lost this awareness. Continual pressures had worn him thin and robbed him of a sense of purpose and meaning.

The Pendulum Swings

I can't help noting the contrast between the picture of Moses in Exodus 18 and the one painted here. In Exodus, we encountered a spiritual superman who believed he could constantly be at it and not fall apart. Now we see a man who has discovered his humanity and his tendency to wear out. Moses is now back to the old image of himself depicted in Exodus 3 and 4. There he felt incapable of performing the task of leading Israel. Now, worn thin by continual and exhausting activity, he is right back there, fully aware of how incapable he is for the task. Only this time, the inadequacy is real and proven.

Moses is not alone in this regard. Many other dedicated servants of God have plunged themselves madly into ministry, forgetting their humanity. Inevitably they begin to wilt under the pressure and fall apart spiritually, physically and emotionally. One author tells the story of Becky, a nurse and Navigators staff member. For seven years she had toiled away at her dual responsibility. Her work included heavy and intense involvement with people. Finally the pressures became too much for her. In her words, "It was a nightmare—except that I was awake...I couldn't sleep, couldn't make decisions, was consistently irritable. One friend said I was like a tooth losing its enamel."[8] Like Moses, Becky seemed to lose her will to live. Her energy and spiritual vigor began to wane. She did not cry out for God to take her life, but inwardly was attracted by the idea of dying: "Although I had no desire to do away with myself, death sounded very good."[9] This is the typical experience of those faithful servants of God who forget their humanity while doing ministry.

I find another contrast between Exodus 18 and Numbers 11:11-15, which represents a shift within Moses. In the former passage, we saw a very unselfish man seeking to meet Israel's needs. In fact, he appeared way too unselfish, too unconcerned about his own physical and emotional needs for his own good. Numbers paints a different picture. Here, the focus shifts to Moses' needs and his own well-being. No longer the self-oblivious prophet, unconcerned about his skin, now Moses only sees his affliction, the crushing burdens and his own wretchedness. Self-interest and self-protection become the dominant themes. No longer is the focus on the people's well-being. Instead, the people have become a great and crushing burden. Before, he seemed to think it quite reasonable to judge the whole people by himself. Now he sings a different tune: "I cannot carry all these people by myself; the burden is too heavy for me." These words hark back to the prophetic voice of Jethro, who warned Moses, "The work is too heavy for you; you cannot handle it alone" (Exodus 18:18b NIV). Prophecy has become reality. What's more, he now sees the imposition of the burden of the people upon him as unreasonable. After all, the people are not his. He did not beget them. His bosom is not large enough to carry them. In these words, Moses lays a charge of irresponsibility at God's door. If he (Moses) did not beget them, who did? The answer is clear. God is the One who birthed Israel. *He* is the One who should bear responsibility for their needs. But instead, He lays *His* responsibility on the back of Moses. How unjust! How unreasonable for God to do such a thing! From

Moses' words, God seems like one of the many irresponsible "deadbeat dads" of our day. They bring kids into the world and then leave them deserted for others to tend.

These contrasts do not surprise me. Remember the Pendulum Principle introduced in chapter 2? Whenever one sees extreme behavior of any sort, one ought to expect its opposite. I have seen similar pendulum swings in those who practice ministry: long periods of over-focus on others, followed by periods of over-focus on one's own needs. We spend long periods of time catering to the needs of others and put our own needs on hold. We secretly believe or hope our day will finally come. When that day doesn't arrive, we begin to lament, "What about my needs? When will someone see and minister to my needs?" That seemed to be Moses lament. It's in these times that we blame God for our condition. We see Him as callously ignoring our needs and we become increasingly angry and resentful toward Him. There is really only one way to avoid this kind of pendulum swing in ministry. Its solution lies in a single word—*balance*. We need to balance serving our own needs with serving the needs of others. If we don't care for our own needs, we take this wild swing where we can no longer see others, only ourselves. It's a wild swing that seeks to compensate for years of self-neglect. When we get there, we lash out at God for not dealing graciously with us. All along the folly was our own.

Environmental Events and Negative Emotions

Before concluding this section on emotions, I should add that negative events in our environment might also serve to unravel us. For example, continual destructive conflict within a congregation may demoralize and wear down ministers and leave them more easily susceptible to emotional turmoil. Similarly, continual exposure to death and trauma may contribute to a minister slowly unraveling. Both situations apply to Moses. These situations may not justify his behaviors, but they do make them more understandable. Though a spiritual giant, Moses was still very human. Being human, he needed emotional outlets to handle these burdens. He needed interludes and time away from the constant demands of ministry to recuperate. There is no evidence in the text that any of this happened.

Without using such intentional strategies, the consequences Moses experienced were all but inevitable.

Several negative experiences appear at the beginning of Numbers 11. The people continued their perpetual pattern of complaining, greatly displeasing God. As spiritual leader, Moses felt compelled to intercede on their behalf. This pattern was nothing new. It characterized the whole journey of Israel: the people complaining and murmuring, the Lord becoming displeased and Moses interceding. This must have engendered a great deal of frustration, as well as spiritual and emotional turmoil. Now, another emotional challenge awaited Moses. This time the people's disobedience reaped a heavy price—God sent fire to consume them. Death was everywhere. Moses now had to grapple with the emotional baggage of deep tragedy and loss. These kinds of burdens can bring the greatest spiritual giant low, and evidently had some impact on Moses. How important it is that we find supportive and sympathetic others with whom we can unburden ourselves!

Behaviors That Reflect Our Spiritual Condition
Giving Up the Call

Given his thinking and his emotions, it's no wonder Moses desired to give up his call. His frustrations troubled him enough that he desired death above the miseries he had encountered. This desire to renounce the call fits with our knowledge of the emotional process of burnout. Research has consistently demonstrated that when people burn out, they tend to relinquish their vocation. That's because burned out individuals become disillusioned and lose a sense of meaning in their work. In addition, the accompanying exhaustion robs individuals of the energy which permits persistence in their calling.

These dynamics certainly apply to ministers. Over the last several years I have had the opportunity to provide interpretation and feedback to clergy using the Adjective Checklist, a psychological test. The Adjective Checklist includes a Well-Being Scale measuring emotional health and stability. Emotional health on this scale largely relates to the ability to respond calmly to stressful situations and form comfortable interpersonal relationships. When scores are low on this scale, it indicates emotional turmoil reflected in self-questioning, self-critical behavior and general feelings of guilt and anxiety. Through reviewing many results on this instrument I see a consistent pattern: in most cases where I encounter low scores on Well-Being, I also see low scores on scales measuring persistence, endurance, productiveness and other task-related behaviors. The conclusion seems clear: guarding one's emotional health through self-care behaviors enhances one's ability to endure, persist and generally respond to ministry's tasks. On the other hand, failing to guard personal well-being diminishes one's ability to persist. No wonder exhausted ministers often seek to give up their call to ministry!

That's exactly what we see in Moses. Stress was high and tolerance low. As a result, he desired to give up the call. Many stressed out and burned out ministers are like Moses in this regard. They may desire to give up ministry but may not make their distaste so glaringly obvious. Some quietly slink away from ministry never to be heard from again. Others make a lateral move into some area perceived as less demanding. For some this move may be appropriate. For others it represents a knowing departure from their call. In many cases, this kind of move places ministers outside their area of giftedness and spells greater difficulties for everyone concerned. Rather than diminishing frustration, they often find it more difficult because they do not serve from their area of strength. At the same time, because they are not especially talented at the new task, they deeply frustrate those with whom they work. Many ministries in the church suffer because of efforts to avoid the area of labor to which we have been called.

Avoiding Spiritual Things

Sometimes, we respond to emotional frustration and burnout by avoiding spiritual things. A pastor at a recent urban summit I attended illustrated this tendency. He told of his efforts to procure and refurbish a place of worship for his congregation. When it was all over he was completely exhausted—physically, emotionally and spiritually. His burned out condition deeply affected his spiritual sensibilities. He developed disgust for the building and hated going to it. He had poured his whole being into the building project, and now he couldn't stand the place.

He had come to abhor the very thing to which he had given himself so untiringly. Some would relate his condition to the phenomenon called "post-building burnout." But his distaste went beyond the building. He also began to struggle with and avoid prayer and other spiritual disciplines.

The avoiding of spiritual things may arise for various reasons. Much of the time burnout is accompanied by depression, leaving us with little energy for any other pursuits, even spiritual ones. The problem is exacerbated by workaholic tendencies in which energy is directed to doing, leaving nothing to address our being. This neglect usually translates into sporadic attention to or downright neglect of spiritual disciplines. As a result, these disciplines do not become cultivated habits in the life of the workaholic minister. They are the first things to fall by the wayside when energies flag.

Sometimes we avoid spiritual things because they remind us of our pain and trauma. Burnout in ministry can lead to deep emotional wounds that traumatize and leave us vulnerable and afraid. We come to fear the things we associate with our burnout. Sometimes the fear may be so great, we begin to avoid those things. That's because every encounter reopens wounds and causes great emotional pain. Since ministers who burn out associate their experience with spiritual things, it's not surprising that they would avoid them. I suspect this was the case with the pastor mentioned earlier. The church building into which he had poured so much of his time and energy reminded him of his pain and trauma. No wonder he wanted to avoid it. I know another minister who shows the same dynamics. He also burned out in ministry. Some eight years later he still struggles with the emotions he experienced in burnout. The emotions are as fresh today as when he burned out and left ministry. Even now, anytime he mentions the experience, the negative feelings quickly and easily rush to the surface. He's right back there experiencing the conflict, the pressure and the trauma associated with his burnout.

Avoiding spiritual things may also signal unresolved issues with God. After all, God stands as the ultimate reality behind spiritual things. Like Moses, we may blame God and hold Him responsible for our pain and suffering. As a result, we may harbor a great deal of anger at God. From this perspective, avoidance of spiritual things may be a veiled way in which we continue to vent our anger towards God. We lack the boldness to speak to God directly about our anger. Instead, we may resort to indirect, passive-aggressive means to demonstrate our boiling anger. We want nothing to do with God or with the things of God.

Yet, there will never be a time when we need contact with God and spiritual things more than when we burn out. It is only through these contacts that we may truly recover from burnout and re-discover ourselves. If we want to return to overall well-being, we need to allow God to walk in our lives in healing ways. It is only through Him that we may experience a restoration of our fractured identity and the confidence decimated in burnout. Burnout is a destructive experience. It destroys our sense of identity. We come to doubt all we believed about ourselves, about our call and our capabilities. We can only have these truly restored through a rediscovery of ourselves in God. He is the One who truly tells us who we are and who accepts us apart from our performance. Besides helping us recover a sense of identity, God is the One who can help us rediscover meaning and significance. In burnout, we lose a sense of the transcendent and, along with it, a sense of meaning and significance. In turn, this loss contributes to the lack of passion and fire we see in burnout. Therefore, to rediscover meaning in ministry, we need to recover the sense of the transcendent—we need to discover God afresh. We need to experience God in ways that reshape our understanding of Him which became distorted in burnout. We need to see Him as the gracious and caring God who loves us and accepts us. Until we discover this, we will never find our way forward. Until we discover the true nature of the God who loves us and calls us, we will never be able to reshape and reframe ministry. It will remain distorted and prone to producing burnout.

Leaving Ministry

Sometimes, avoiding spiritual things simply does not give enough distance, so ministers leave ministry entirely. This difference between those who avoid and those who leave may serve a diagnostic purpose. Those who avoid may have experienced a lesser degree of trauma than those who leave.

Retreating from sacred things allows the avoiders the time and distance necessary for healing. In time they may recover and return to their former spiritual activities. Those who leave may be different. They have been so deeply scarred they find it difficult to return to ministry even after they have had time and distance. Time and distance brings no healing. They have been so devastated, so totally disillusioned and traumatized, they find it unbearable to ever enter ministry again.

Leaving ministry does not necessarily mean the minister gives up on God. I know one former pastor who experienced tremendous difficulties in ministry. These pressures eventually led to his burnout and retreat from ministry. Although he has maintained a vital relationship with God, he has continued to shun pastoral ministry altogether. It's as though ministry traumatized him to such a degree that he fears getting close to pastoral ministry, lest he gets burned again. He has found other ways to stay close to the work of the kingdom. However, the avenues he chooses have been far below his level of education, training and capabilities. Apparently, he has chosen to work below his abilities rather than face again the pressures, frustration and potential trauma ministry brought.

Some ministers display a flair for the dramatic when giving up the call to ministry. Spiritually fractured, some may engage in crazy, escapist behaviors. Remember the pastor we encountered at the beginning of this book, who faked suicide to avoid the stress that was overtaking his life? One must wonder if these outrageous acts are simply different manifestations of our anger and resentment towards God. In this way of thinking, they represent unconscious ways in which we continue to blame God for our troubles. I know this is not always true, but I suspect it sometimes is. However we understand these behaviors, we clearly see how they mimic Moses' desire in the text. He might not have demonstrated his desire with crazy behavior, but his desire for death had a craziness all its own. This crazy aspect, at least in part, demonstrates the lengths to which desperate, burned out ministers will go.

Carnaling Out

Sometimes, burnout in ministry leads to outright sins of the flesh. The term "carnaling out" has been coined to describe the misconduct that sometimes characterizes those who have burned out. Some involve themselves in illicit affairs, even with parishioners. The growing number of incidents of sexual misconduct in the parish seems to point to increasing levels of stress within the lives of ministers. At other times, stress and the burnout accompanying it may show its presence when ministers take to the bottle and become raging alcoholics.

This tying of sinful behaviors to stress and burnout is not an attempt to excuse sin. However, I say it to make a point: the pressures, stresses and resulting burnout may serve to weaken spiritual sensibilities. Those sensibilities are like a spiritual immune system. Using this analogy, stress and burnout are like diseases that attack our spiritual immune system, leaving us vulnerable and much more susceptible to indulging in sinful behaviors. Having our spiritual sensibilities dulled, we find ourselves more likely to say and do things we would never have imagined. Who could have imagined that Moses would break out in this display of anger at God? But, weakened by stress and frustration, he did. The same is true for us. The pressures of ministry can serve to weaken us spiritually and make us more open to yielding to the constant temptations of our enemy, Satan.

The Loss of Faith

The ultimate consequence in burnout is the complete erosion of one's spiritual life. Ministers sometimes burn out so completely that they develop a thorough disillusionment with God and spiritual things. When this happens, they may relinquish all semblance of the spiritual in their lives and lose their relationship with God. That's a perennial hazard for those who labor in ministry. Paul knew this well. He was well aware that while seeking to preach and save others, he himself could be a castaway (I Corinthians 9:27). Apparently, Richard Baxter had the same thing in mind when he cautioned pastors:

> See that the work of saving grace be thoroughly wrought in your own souls. Take heed to yourselves, lest you be void of that saving grace of God which

you offer to others, and be strangers to the effectual working of that gospel which you preach; and lest, while you proclaim to the world the necessity of a Savior, your own hearts should neglect him, and you should miss of an interest in him and his saving benefits. Take heed to yourselves, lest you perish, while you call upon others to take heed of perishing; and lest you famish yourselves while you prepare food for them.[10]

What a tragedy it is when zealous ministers pour out their souls in serving others, only to lose their own souls in the process. This represents the ultimate spiritual consequence of serving from the Moses Model.

1. Kathy O'Reilly, "Burnout: The Elijah Syndrome," *World Christian* 6:2 (March/April, 1987): p. 26.
2. Matthew Henry, *Commentary on the Whole Bible, Condensed Version* (Albany, OR: Ages Software, 1995), p. 218.
3. Laurie Ann Pearlman and Karen W. Saakvitne, "Treating therapists with vicarious traumatization and secondary traumatic stress disorders," *Compassion Fatigue*, ed. Charles R. Figley (New York: Brunner/Mazel, 1995), p. 161.
4. Cary Cherniss, *Beyond Burnout: Helping Teachers, Nurses, Therapists and Lawyers Recover from Stress and Disillusionment* (New York: Routledge, 1995).
5. Ibid., pp. 37, 39-41.
6. Dean R. Hoge and Jacqueline E. Wenger, *Pastors in Transition: Why Clergy Leave Local Church Ministry* (Grand Rapids, MI: Eerdmans, 2005). p. 36, 100. The authors noted denominational conflict and other factors as a reason for leaving ministry. For example, 54% of UMC ministers who left indicated a lack of denominational support. Another 63% indicated the inability to speak openly and honestly with denominational officials.
7. Christine Maslach, *Burnout: The Cost of Caring* (Englewood Cliffs, NJ: Prentice Hall, Inc., 1982).
8. Ibid., pp. 26-27.
9. Ibid., p. 27.
10. Richard Baxter, *The Reformed Pastor*, abr. William Brown (Albany, OR: Ages Software, 1995), p. 17.

Chapter 5

Old Frames for Doing Ministry

I met "Rev. John" a few years ago in a doctor of ministry course. A few weeks after the class ended, he sent me a copy of an article that had appeared in a local newspaper. The article documented his experience with burnout and his subsequent recovery. Rev. John became acutely aware of his difficulties one Sunday afternoon during a family outing. That afternoon, he suffered a full-blown panic attack. The attack served as the climax to a number of symptoms he had experienced. Leading up to this event, he had noticed a general loss of energy and optimism, though no one would have known it. John had mastered the art of putting on a smiling face for his staff and congregation and functioned well from his clergy persona. But often in the safety of his home he would break down and weep. The panic attack that October afternoon convinced him he needed help. Within 24 hours, he had talked with several persons about his condition. He conferred with his wife, his father, his district superintendent and a counselor. His district superintendent quickly and insightfully intervened and arranged a three-month medical leave with full salary and benefits. With time and diligent care, Rev. John slowly recovered and regained much of his optimism, energy and vision.[1] He was one of the lucky ones.

What got Rev. John into trouble in the first place? In his own words, his difficulties revolved around his increasing busyness and a failure to care for himself. Though constantly available to others, he was mostly unavailable to himself. After 12 years in pastoral ministry, he had become entrenched in a life of busyness. This made it "...very easy not to deal with things that I needed for my emotional well-being." His life gradually teetered out of balance. "I rarely had down time....It's not that I never went golfing or that kind of thing, but if I did I would go golfing and come home to do something else. I never set out intentionally to be so busy that I wouldn't take care of myself, but it just happened. And I think over a period of time of doing that I just wore out any emotional reserves that I had."[2]

Stories like Rev. John's abound. Few are marked with the understanding, grace and redemption evident in his story. One would think these familiar tales would inspire new ways of thinking about and practicing ministry. From my experience this is not the case. Even though we see the negative toll such thinking inflicts, many ministers still practice the same old styles. Many of us still demonstrate habits promoting neglect of ourselves and those we love. These unhealthy approaches seem deeply entrenched in our psyches. They are like deadly tentacles securely holding us in their clutches, making it virtually impossible to break free from their influence. Old frames of thinking about and practicing ministry seem like bad genes transmitted across generations. We may not like the physical and emotional consequences but we cannot seem to shake free from their influence. Why do negative ways of thinking and practicing ministry still prevail? I see several reasons which contribute to our entrenched habits. These reasons form the basis for this chapter.

The Example of Biblical Figures

Biblical figures and the examples they set greatly influence our approach to ministry. Stalwarts of the faith like Moses and Elijah provide models for ministry that many of us seek to emulate. Because we highly revere such giants of the faith, we often do not adequately critique their methods. In fact, we avoid any form of critique. I became acutely aware of this tendency a few years ago in a writing class. I had proposed writing about and critiquing the Moses Model for doing ministry. The class professor was a prolific writer fully aware of all of the dynamics related to publishing. He warned that I would have to be careful how I wrote about Moses. Because Moses is held in such high esteem, he felt casting him in a negative light would meet with quick rejection. The same arguments could be made against writing about the great prophet Elijah. Both men were spiritual giants and great servants of God. We look at them and justifiably see heroes of the faith who, in many respects, are worthy of emulation. But sometimes we take this to an extreme and ignore some of the glaring problems in their approach to ministry.

I suspect their spiritual greatness partly contributes to the problem. We may falsely believe that everything associated with them is spiritual and good. Blinded by spiritual greatness, we too quickly gloss over glaring problems which God does not intend for us to imitate. I have seen a similar hesitancy in critiquing other great servants of God. I have found this hesitancy within my own tradition as it relates to John Wesley. In some circles, there is an aversion to saying anything critical about this great man of God. I know a situation where a student asked a professor about John Wesley's married life. The professor rather quickly dismissed the question as though it had little relevance. The student never got an answer. Yet the question was an honest one that could have gleaned valuable information on how one functions as a minister in a troubled marriage.

Fortunately, God is not so easily blinded by the greatness of His servants. He can laud them and still exert good judgment in pointing out their flaws when appropriate. God even uses negative events in their lives to teach us fresh truth. He calls us to be like Him in this regard. We can revere and justly pay tribute to greatness, but we must never be blinded by the glitter and thereby miss valuable lessons.

Once we remove the scales of admiration from our eyes, we can see and learn from the mistakes of examples like Moses and Elijah. Despite their obvious spiritual greatness, both men demonstrated a style of ministry with severe negative consequences. One author labels the latter's ministry style the "Elijah Syndrome."[3] In Elijah, we see how exhaustion and isolation from community can lead to self-deception and depression that brings a desire for one's own demise. We see a very similar phenomenon in Moses. His exhaustion led to a similar problem and similar desire for death. In this book, I have used the Moses Model to describe this same approach to ministry. Significantly, God also saw problems with their ministry styles and sought to correct these saintly giants.

Bad Modeling

Besides biblical figures, bad role models from life and experience have negatively influenced our approach to ministry. As much as I hate to say it, in my formative years in ministry, I encountered ministers who modeled approaches similar to that of Moses. They advocated in word and deed an approach which ignored personal and family needs. Much of this was well-intentioned. Like Boyd Larsen, mentioned earlier, they were driven by a sense of urgency. They felt they needed to save the world and had limited time to do it. In the process, they cut short their own ministry because of self-abuse. But it's not just ministers who mentored us that instilled bad habits. Consultants, gurus and other experts sometimes err by advocating a similar style. Elsewhere in this book, I mentioned an example provided by John Ortberg. According to him, one church-planting consultant advised a group of pastors they would have to pay the price of a successful church plant. The consultant meant they should do whatever was necessary, including allowing their marriages to suffer and putting their children on hold. That's just "collateral damage" that comes with building the kingdom.[4] Tragically, many of us seem to believe that God approves this sort of strategy. Perhaps that's why this kind of thinking is so appealing to so many.

Sometimes clergy educators unintentionally give the same impression by words and example. One of my early professors suggested burnout was a preferable alternative to rustout. Indeed, this self-destructive style was presented as the path the committed minister should follow. Not every clergy educator is so shortsighted, but few of us are without fault when it comes to the overly sacrificial images we project about ministry.

The Burden of Expectations

Lofty expectations fuel exhausting approaches to ministry. Sometimes the expectations are self-imposed. We sometimes set unrealistic expectations reaching perfectionist proportions that no human could possibly meet. I have met some who labored under such expectation. Even when they had done their best, they still couldn't be content. They constantly felt inward pressure to push for greater results. A pervasive dissatisfaction with their efforts and accomplishments fueled their quest. Yet they tended to judge their accomplishments unrealistically. Their judgments often possessed a fictional quality, based as it was on their own feelings of failure. The feelings were largely fueled by messages of inadequacy from the past, not actual facts. Not surprisingly, they undervalued their achievements in ways that would mystify the objective onlooker. These perfectionist ministers were often not aware of their conspiracy against themselves. Blinded to their own lack of realistic appraisals, they tended to set higher and higher expectations which eventually crippled them and their ministry.

Having said this, one cannot ignore the role church leaders and congregations play in keeping ministers locked into wrong frames for doing ministry. Many times leaders and congregations bring a myriad of expectations which shackle pastors. One pastor noted, "A pastor needs to do too many things well in order for the church to prosper, including administration, biblical scholarship, counseling, youth work and pastoral calling. The results are either a dysfunctional family life or divorce at home."[5] The clergy spouse also experiences the burden of these expectations. One pastor's spouse noted, "We wear so many hats. From our family we provide preaching, directing the choir, pianist, special music. Sunday School teachers, bookkeeper, ladies' ministries, and many more. Burnout from sheer physical exhaustion is just around the corner most of the time."[6] These expectations rise exponentially for those touted as rising stars. Leaders often expect them to produce great results in a quick space of time. I have seen rising stars who quickly ascended to their zenith, only to quickly fall with no light left—burned out and useless to themselves or to the church. They became victims of the burdensome expectations placed on them. In trying to live up these impossible expectations, they exhausted themselves.

Even our culture plays a role in our workaholic tendencies. In an interview with *Leadership* magazine, Henri Nouwen reflected on the role culture plays in ministers' workaholic habits: "Culture tells us...do as much as you can or you'll never make it."[7] Unfortunately, we sometimes hear the voice of culture louder than we hear the voice of God. Our culture tells us to define our worth and usefulness by performance and productivity. God paints a whole different picture. He counts us worthwhile simply because we are His creatures and because of our relationship with Him. Ultimately, Nouwen was right. He suggested we cannot fight the demons of busyness directly. We will find it difficult to continually say no to the multiple demands made upon us unless we find something ten times more attractive. For Nouwen, the most attractive thing is radical intimacy with God.

A Western Model of Spirituality

In his book, *In His Spirit: A Guide to Today's Spirituality*, Richard J. Hauser provides a model which explains some of these difficulties. He contrasts two models of spirituality—a *scriptural model* versus a *Western model* of spirituality. For Hauser, an adequate understanding of the self lies at the heart of Christian spirituality. Thus he defines spirituality as "...our effort with grace to become what we have been created by the Lord to be."[8] These two approaches to spirituality represent alternate paths to self-discovery. The scriptural approach seeks to discover the self in God. The Western model of spirituality discovers the self outside God; that is, through one's own efforts.

According to Hauser, this latter approach to spirituality is not explicitly articulated, but its assumptions deeply affect our understanding and living of the Christian life. In my opinion, these assumptions also deeply affect our understanding and practice of ministry. As I see it, the Western model and its assumptions help to frame ministry in a manner that inevitably poses problems.[9] In essence, espousing this model leads to an unscriptural and rigid understanding of ministry which creates all kinds of difficulties. This model poses a greater danger because it is largely an unconscious, implicit model. Because it is not explicit, we tend to follow its assumptions more unconsciously than consciously. Like a child carefully indoctrinated and trained to follow parental injunctions without question, we follow its precepts unthinkingly without investigating its actual impact on our personal lives and practice. Not surprisingly, few of us who practice this model can say how we adopted it. But the telltale signs of its presence appear in all that we do. It's like we picked it up as we would some harmful virus. Once inside us, it secretly works to produce disastrous results. It is this unconscious, unthinking adherence to the model that makes it so dangerous to the practice of ministry and the minister's well-being.

How does the Western model of spirituality shape the understanding and practice of ministry? I see its influence in five key areas:

1. It distorts beliefs about God and the role of the Spirit as it relates to ministry.
2. It promotes in ministers a false basis for understanding themselves and the formation of their identity.
3. It engenders an individualistic approach to ministry that neglects or ignores the role of community.
4. It leads to an understanding of ministry that places human activity at the center and relegates God to a marginal role.
5. It elevates doing above being and orients one to a ministry largely focused on performance and rewards.

These distortions mutually influence each other. Together they keep ministers locked into a style of ministry which slowly wears them out. Given their importance, these errors need some discussion. I begin with the misunderstandings regarding God and the role of the Holy Spirit inherent in the Western model. Though I agree with Hauser that misunderstanding ourselves is a key error we make, misunderstanding God is even more foundational. If our theology is flawed, our anthropology will be flawed, along with everything else.

Misunderstanding God

The Western model depicts God as residing in heaven, separate from human affairs. It emphasizes God's transcendence to such a degree that it excludes His immanence. Its portrayal of God is essentially deistic. God has set the world in motion but takes a hands-off approach in ongoing human affairs. How different from the scriptural view of God! In Scripture, God is always active in human affairs. Given this basic misunderstanding of God, we are not surprised to find that this model fosters misunderstanding of the Holy Spirit's work within the lives of individuals and in ministry. In fact, this model sees the Holy Spirit as outside the human spirit. He does not work within individuals to purify and empower them. What's more, He certainly does not work in ministry. Ministry does not depend on the gifts of the Holy Spirit. Rather, ministry becomes a purely human activity devoid of the Spirit and the Spirit's gifts. It relies on human motivation and native human abilities.

Most ministers do not consciously or intellectually hold to these beliefs about God and the Holy Spirit. It's not an explicit model carefully reasoned. Rather, it is held at an unconscious level, defying logic and real-world data. We most often encounter it indirectly in negative feelings and driven behaviors. An example from clinical practice might make my meaning clearer. I once encountered an individual whom most people would consider bright and intelligent. His academic achievements amply documented his ability. He had graduated summa cum laude and had completed a graduate degree in business with almost a 4.0 average. Yet this individual could never believe that he was smart. He actually thought he was stupid. In terms of the evidence, this belief was more fiction than fact. But he held to this belief tenaciously, attributing his success to luck or sheer persistence, never intelligence. It later became evident that this belief had been etched into his being by a father who constantly berated him for stupidity. This falsehood became his unreasoned truth which no amount of real-world evidence could dislodge. It deeply shaped his feelings of inferiority. Moreover, it led to an impulse-driven behavior to be constantly self-effacing and to detract from his accomplishments.

Ministers hold these beliefs about God and ministry in a similar manner. Early formative experiences and modeling by ministers they admired sent such beliefs deep into their being. Such beliefs about God and the practice of ministry were not to be reasoned but lived out. Perhaps you have met ministers who by their style give evidence to holding such views. They act as if ministry were totally up to them. They labor as though they are indispensable and that without them ministry would ultimately fail. They rely more on their native abilities than the gifts of the Spirit. By their behaviors they loudly declare God afar off, totally separated from their everyday world of ministry. And so they constantly drive themselves, paying little heed to their own well-being. Besides their driven behavior, one also often finds negative emotions that make no sense given real-world data.

Pastor John was like that. In his years of ministry he had achieved a great deal. He had planted new churches and had seen them grow tremendously. He had won awards and accolades from his peers who recognized his abilities and gifts. Everyone recognized his abilities but Pastor John. He was constantly plagued with the terrible feeling that he had not done enough, yet he could not identify its source. Moreover, he constantly devalued his success. In his head, he knew this evaluation did not match the facts. But he could never transfer the truth from his head to his heart. Because he could not, he could never rest in ministry. He had to keep pushing to do and to accomplish more. It was all up to him. No sooner had he finished one task than he rushed to start another. His theology of ministry, framed out of an unconscious Western model, was alive and well. I once told him that God affirmed him and was pleased with his commitment to ministry. As he heard these words, the tears began to stream down his face. But even then he found it difficult to identify the reason for his feelings. He was accustomed to doing, but seemed to have lost touch with his need for positive feelings of affirmation. He lived out of a false guilt that constantly pushed him to do more. If I had asked Pastor John about his theology of God, he likely would have intellectually disavowed and refuted any deistic understandings of God relating to ministry. He would have likely affirmed ministry as dependent on God, not him. But his driven behavior in ministry told a different story.

This discrepancy may surprise some, but it shouldn't. There is often a big difference between the theology we hold in our heads and that which we practice in our lives. Some of us practice a theology that is far below what we hold to intellectually. For instance, most of us hold to the idea of a God of grace, but when it comes to the practice of ministry, we act like God is some ungracious tyrant whipping us to produce bricks from straw. We perceive God as never satisfied with our efforts, pronouncing our every attempt as "not good enough." Likewise, we may intellectually believe that ministry is empowered by the Holy Spirit, but act as though it largely depends on our efforts to produce results.

The impact of this view of God should not be under-estimated. We can emphasize God's transcendence to such a degree that we lose His immanent presence in our lives and ministry. Perhaps it is this emphasis which contributes to the problems of intimacy with God evident in the lives of some ministers. One cannot very well be intimate with an absent God. Neither should we expect the power and presence of an absent God to be evident in our ministries. Intimacy, power and presence can only come from a God who is near.

The Loss of the Transcendent in Ministry

But the neglect of God's presence is only half the story. *Losing* a sense of the transcendent God can also contribute to a loss of meaning in ministry. Loss of meaning plays a prominent role in burnout. In *Beyond Burnout*, Cary Cherniss argues that burnout is not really a disease of overcommitment. He suggests that those who burn out may be overinvolved in their work, but are not committed in a moral sense. Rather, he sees their commitment as egoistic since it springs from their need to derive self-esteem based on their performance. For Cherniss, one can only be morally committed when the latter is based "…on a belief in something [or, as I would say, some*one*] greater than themselves. It was transcendent."[10] Belief must be in something transcendent if one is to be inoculated against burnout. Commitment to something transcendent provides persons with a sense of meaning. Individuals do not become emotionally exhausted when they engage in meaningful work. In support, Cherniss pointed to nuns who worked in a potentially exhausting environment but did not become burned out. They had found supreme meaning in laboring for God. But when we work from a Western model of spirituality, we have largely lost the transcendent God in our ministry. In fact, ministry can largely become a labor to discover our identity rather than a labor of love for God's sake. No wonder many ministers experience a loss of passion and burnout! We have not discovered Someone greater than ourselves.

Identity Formation

Trying to discover self on our own terms is a major part of the problem. In the Western model of spirituality, the quest is to discover the self outside of God. Given the deistic views of God, this approach to self-discovery makes sense. An absent God has no legitimate role to play in the human quest for identity. With no God to guide our efforts, we must carve out our identity through our own efforts and performance. Even a spiritual activity like ministry may become another avenue to serve our private quest for self-discovery. In contrast, the scriptural model offers a whole new approach. We discover ourselves, not from our own efforts and performance, but through an intimate relationship with God. Out of this intimacy, His Spirit becomes joined to our spirit and provides the basis for the truest discovery of the self. It's a discovery grounded in the certain knowledge that God loves us for ourselves, not simply because of what we do.[11]

By our habits, we ministers demonstrate that we unwittingly follow the Western model as a way to determine our identity. Many of us spend a great deal of time feverishly performing as a means to establish our identities. We hope to establish our worth by our efforts and productivity. What's more, we want others to recognize our talents and worth. Unfortunately, this approach often leads to great frustration. Instead of coming to a solid identity, endless activity sometimes causes us to question our worth. It's as though we have bought fool's gold. We set out to discover our identity in our activities. Instead, after we have paid with our energy and efforts, we discover we still do not know who we are and that our identity is more fractured than before. That's because work is a false basis for discovering our truest selves. Such efforts never lead to a fixed and secure sense of self. Any benefit derived from our efforts is fleeting. In order to reinforce our self-esteem, we must continue to produce. We can never rest secure in past efforts. As soon as we complete one task successfully, we must move to another task to maintain the sense of self previously gained. In a sense, this futile search for the self through work efforts is like being on drugs. The drug addict seeks to produce a high through the use of a drug. But to maintain the high, the addict must continue to use the drug to maintain the feeling. In fact, to maintain a similar level of the high, the addict needs the drug in greater quantities. Seeking one's identity through work is like that. It never lasts and it takes increasingly more work production to maintain that momentary feeling of being a worthwhile person. It is workaholic behavior designed to serve the addict's need for a self-esteem high.

The Loss of Community

Because ministry sometimes deteriorates into an effort at self-discovery, it can become a solitary activity cutting us off from community. We spend so much time focusing on individual achievement and accolades, we have little time left for community. We thereby lose touch with ministry as a spiritual activity that takes place in a community of faith. That missing dimension can wreak havoc in our lives as time goes on.

The ancient prophet Elijah provides a good biblical example of the negative impact of a loss of community. His isolation brought dire consequences. Though a search for personal identity did not inspire him, his zeal drove him in a solitary direction, nonetheless. It effectively cut him off from the community of faith remaining in Israel. Isolation's negative impact did not appear when he confronted the prophets of Baal on Mt. Carmel. This was the height of his success. We rarely sense our need for others at the apex of achievement. Success is often an experience that blesses aloneness as a desirable thing. It's so much easier to bask in the limelight alone. It's a whole different story when we encounter failure and frustration. At those times we feel our aloneness acutely. It's then that we desire the comfort of human companionship. Those times finally came to Elijah. Terrorized by Jezebel's threats, he came to feel the absence of community profoundly. We see this in his lament: "I am the only one left and now they are trying to kill me too." (1 Kings 19:10b, 14b). These words proclaim his isolation and its devastating effect on his fragile psyche. They also attest to the unreality that sets in once we separate ourselves from others. We may come to believe things that aren't true at all, or are true only in our skewed perceptions. Elijah was *not* the only one left. In fact, according to God, he had reserved 7,000 in Israel who had not bowed to Baal. But this was not Elijah's reality.

An unfortunate outcome of aloneness is that it leaves us without anyone to interpret our social reality. Elijah needed this kind of correction. He needed someone to correct his skewed perceptions of reality exacerbated by emotional and mental confusion. Ayala Pines and company have suggested the interpretation of social reality is one aspect of social support.[12] Much of the time God provides contact with kindred spirits to help us interpret reality. Sometimes those persons help us stand firm when our perceptions are right. But we also need persons who question our false "realities." Elijah needed that. But, bereft of social contacts, God had to do this for him.

But that's not all. Elijah's loneliness also left him without persons who could provide both emotional support and emotional challenge. He needed sympathetic souls around him who could stand with him in his hour of fear and discouragement. He also needed the emotional challenge that brought him out of his deep emotional funk. God's design is that we experience this support from real-life people who offer us the grace of listening, and provide both sympathetic and challenging speech when appropriate.

Elijah's situation highlights another truth relative to clergy's sense of isolation. His situation raises the possibility that great feats for God and the accompanying success may isolate us from others. Sometimes individual success leads us to believe we are something special, distinct and separate from less-achieving brethren. I have sometimes seen this phenomenon at ministerial gatherings where clergy seemed segregated by their status. There appeared to be a kind of "sacred pecking order." Pastors of highly successful churches (measured numerically) tended to gather together. Pastors of less successful churches gathered in their own little corner with less successful brethren like themselves. At least that's the way it often appeared to me. But sometimes it is not successful persons who segregate themselves. Sometimes others, intimidated by that success, keep themselves at a respectful distance. Unless we exert a great deal of care, our success in ministry may make us strangers to the community of faith. Whatever the reason, loss of community erodes the basis by which personal commitment is sharpened. When we lack community, all that remains is an egoistic commitment that cannot withstand the difficulties and stresses in ministry. In the face of this onslaught, we sometimes quickly crumble and fade away.

Ministry That Marginalizes God

As implied in the previous pages, the Western model of spirituality fosters an understanding of ministry that marginalizes God. Ministry becomes an activity, motivated and enabled by human intention and ability. This stance represents a radical departure from a scriptural understanding of ministry. Scripturally, God calls and empowers persons for ministry. Their task is to graciously respond. In the Western model, the tables get turned around. It is humans who initiate ministry. They don't need God's call to practice ministry. They might choose it as easily as one chooses any other career. In this model, the call to ministry is a purely natural call inspired by human desires, inclinations and natural abilities. What's more, performance in ministry does not depend upon the Holy Spirit's power and gifting; human effort and talent are sufficient. We have all it takes to successfully pursue ministry under our own power. We are the ones who must expend effort and energy to perform ministry. We become the indispensable persons upon which ministry rises and falls. If we don't do it all, it never gets done. Such a system leaves little place for God. We only need God to rubber-stamp our efforts and reward us when we have finished with our work.[13]

What's more, this approach focuses largely on the competence and control of the professional minister. Competence and control are all we need to function effectively. We are no different than any other profession. We may dabble in spiritual things, but largely rely on our natural means to achieve spiritual ends. Personal spiritual qualifications are either ignored or minimized. That's unfortunate! Spiritual credentials may not be necessary in other areas of endeavor, but are absolutely essential in the practice of ministry. By making this emphasis, I do not argue against competence in ministerial skills. Competence is necessary, but it is not enough. More than anything else, ministers need to be firmly grounded in God.

Unfortunately, ministry initiated and maintained by human inclinations and abilities has some unfortunate repercussions. For one, we may surrender it as easily as we once chose it. If we become too stressed and too frustrated, we can choose to give it all up. There's no need to consult God. It's all up to us from beginning to end. What a far cry from those who believe God called them to ministry. The prophet Jeremiah felt God's call. That call kept him grounded even in the midst of derision and persecution. At times he wanted to give it all up, but the call kept him steady. And so he could proclaim, "But if I say, 'I will not mention Him or speak any more in His name,' His word is in my heart like a fire, a fire shut up in my bones. I am weary of holding it in; indeed, I cannot" (Jeremiah 20:9 NIV). The call kept him preaching in God's name in spite of his troubles. Without this call to steady us, we are likely to surrender our call when things get rough. Without God's sustaining power we have little motivation to hang in there when difficulties arise. This is true for at least two reasons. First, without God we are devoid of His motivation that keeps us grounded in times of frustration. Moreover, we have no spiritual source on which to draw strength for continued endurance. We lack the spiritual resources which provide a means of support and encouragement. Second, without God the source of ultimate meaning for participating in ministry is largely absent. We serve in our own name, not in the name of One who is bigger than we are.

Performance and Rewards

Needless to say, the Western model highlights the *doing* of ministry as the ultimate thing. That's why ministers who unconsciously serve from this model focus so much on achieving results and performing. Doing is everything! Performance is where it's at! Everything else is either unimportant or secondary, at best. Little, if any, place is given to the *being*—the personal formation that underlies ministry. I suspect many of us choose this model because we are most comfortable with activity. Activity is something into which we can sink our teeth. On the other hand, it's hard for us to get our hands and minds around this "being" thing. It's so intangible and difficult to gauge.

Besides, when we perform, we expect reward. Sometimes we seek reward in attention and adulation from others. Ministry then becomes compromised because we are constantly looking over our shoulder to ensure the right people are noticing our efforts and achievements. Unfortunately, no amount of attention and adulation ever really meets our need. I recently spoke to one pastor who confirmed this. The attention and adulation felt good for a while, but its effects quickly waned. In fact, this minister often found it difficult to accept fully the attention and adulation he was receiving from others. How ironic! Gaining the attention of others was a big part of his motivation, but when it came he could not fully accept it or enjoy it.

Ultimately, we look for rewards from God. We long to hear His voice saying, "Well done, thou good and faithful servant!" But even here we are sometimes disappointed. Just as we sometimes find it difficult to accept attention from others, I have found a similar thing when it comes to God. I have encountered ministers who labored to achieve great things for God, and yet believed God was displeased with their efforts. They still perceived Him condemning their efforts. This does not mean God will not be faithful to reward those who labor for Him. But I sometimes wonder if some of us will be disappointed. Matthew 7:21-23 readily comes to mind: "Not everyone who says to me, 'Lord, Lord,' will enter the kingdom of heaven, but only he who does the will of my Father who is in heaven. Many will say to me on that day, 'Lord, Lord, did we not prophesy in your name, and in your name drive out demons and perform many miracles?' Then I will tell them plainly, 'I never knew you. Away from me, you evildoers!'" (NIV). Here it was a matter of the ultimate reward—entry into the kingdom. But these individuals touted their performance—the things they did in His name—as the basis for receiving the reward. Christ reasoned on a far different basis. His established basis involved relationship, not results; being, not doing. They were disqualified for the prize because, while chasing results, they failed to know Him. Perhaps in this saying there is a word even for those who know Him. Perhaps in this saying there is a word even for those who know him. It's not simply about performance and results; it's about an intimate knowledge of Jesus Christ. Get this central truth right and the rest will fall in line.

1. Judy Tarjanyi, "Help in Avoiding and Treating Clergy Burnout," *The Blade, Toledo, Ohio,* January 15, 2000. Used with permission. I have changed the name of the pastor.

2. Ibid., p. 5.

3. Kathy O'Reilly, "Burnout: The Elijah Syndrome," *World Christian* 6:2 (March/April, 1987), p. 26.

4. John Ortberg, "What's Really Behind Our Fatigue?" *Leadership* 18:2 (Spring 1997): p. 108-113 at 108.

5. H.B. London and Neil B.Wiseman, *Pastors at Risk* (Wheaton, IL: Victor Books, 1993), p. 55.

6. Ibid.

7. Leadership editors, "Deepening Our Conversation with God: An interview with Richard Foster and Henri Nouwen," *Leadership* 18:1 (Winter 1997): p. 112-118 at 114.

8. Richard J. Hauser, *In His Spirit: A Guide to Today's Spirituality* (New York: Paulist Press, 1982), p. 5.

9. Norman Shawchuck and Roger Heuser, *Leading the Congregation: Caring for Yourself while Serving the People* (Nashville: Abingdon, 1993). See Chapter 9, pp. 119-138. The authors also see the Western model as affecting ministry.

10. Cary Cherniss, *Beyond Burnout: Helping Teachers, Nurses, Therapists and Lawyers Recover from Stress and Disillusionment* (New York: Routledge, 1995), p. 185.

11. Donald Hands and Wayne L. Fehr, *Spiritual Wholeness for Clergy: A New Psychology of Intimacy with God, Self and Others* (Washington, D.C.: Alban Institute, 1993), p. 55.

12. Ayala Pines, Elliot Aronson and Ditsa Kafry, *Burnout* (New York: The Free Press, 1981), p. 128-129, 131. Also, Ayala Pines and Elliot Aronson, *Career Burnout, Causes and Cures* (New York: The Free Press, 1988).

13. Hauser, *In His Spirit*, pp. 9-13.

Chapter 6

The Importance of Being Human

"A very large amount of human suffering and frustration is caused by the fact that men and women are not content to be the sort of beings that God made them but try to persuade themselves that they are really beings of some different kind."[1] E. L. Mascall wrote these words many years ago, but they still possess the ring of truth. Mascall spoke about the tendency of humans to either think too highly or too lowly about their nature. Sometimes we consider ourselves nothing more than "a superior grade of mammal." At other times, we think we are pure spirits and deem our physical nature irrelevant. In either case, we cause ourselves immense difficulties and pain because we do not truly know our nature.

Mascall spoke about humans in general, but his words could easily apply to ministers. Ministers have gained notoriety for trying to live like "beings of some different kind." We sometimes act as though we are superhuman. We often seek to shed our finite, human garb for the clothing of supernatural beings. Like mild-mannered Clark Kent, we appear human, but hearing desperate cries for help, we quickly find some back alley in which to shed our human attire and emerge as super-pastors ready for the rescue. Sometimes we attempt a rescue when the person evidently does not wish to be saved.

The attempt to live beyond our nature springs from illusion. We are not superhuman. Not even close! We merely try to live like we are. The illusion holds great deceptive power over us. We must constantly struggle to separate fact from fiction: we serve in the name of God, but we are not gods. We are not messiahs; we are creatures, not the Creator. When we forget this truth, we often strive to live outside our boundaries. Inevitably, we suffer the consequences of continued suffering and frustration.

Because of the power of this divine illusion, we need constant reminders of our identity. God seeks to do just that. In a variety of ways He seeks to remind us of our finitude and the fact that He has bounded us with all kinds of limits. That's why Genesis has so much to teach us. In the creation narrative we can discover anew the true fabric of our lives. There we learn something about the boundaries that frame our human existence. If we live within these boundaries, we generally do well. When we forget these limitations, we bring upon ourselves unnecessary pain.

In the last few years, I have started using a video narration of the biblical creation account in clergy stress management seminars. My reason for doing this is simple: I believe that going back to our foundations can provide us with information about our true identity. I have been pleasantly surprised how readily ministers grasp the truths in that narrative. They easily perceive the principles for self-care inherent in creation. Moreover, they quickly realize how these principles apply to the practice of ministry. Hopefully, this knowledge and appreciation of our human identity will help us reframe ourselves as we pursue the practice of ministry. As a result, we will likely engage ministry with a different style: one that allows us to be human and cater to those needs while pursuing our call. That's what this chapter is all about. It's all about rediscovering our unique human identity and its implications for reframing ministry.

The Height of God's Creation

Humans hold a special place in the created order. In some circles, that's not a fashionable thing to say. Some would have us believe we are nothing more than a mass of protoplasm. To them, we differ very little from the animals. Genesis and the Bible present a different message. Consider the ancient psalmist's amazement regarding the special place humans hold:

> When I consider your heavens, the work of your fingers, the moon and the stars, which you have set in place, what is man that you are mindful of him, the son of man that you care for him? You made him a little lower than the heavenly beings and crowned him with glory and honor. You made him ruler over the works of your hands; you put everything under his feet: all flocks and herds, and the beasts of the

field, the birds of the air, and the fish of the sea, all
that swim the paths of the seas (Psalm 8:3-8 NIV).

The psalmist obviously agreed with the writer of Genesis:
humans represent the crowning achievement of God's creative
activity. We find this truth implicit in several places in the
creation narrative. The early acts of creation seem like the
activities of a gracious host preparing to welcome honored
guests. So, after fashioning a hospitable and beautiful world,
God created humans. This image alone should signal our special
value to God.

Other features of the narrative set humans apart from the rest
of the created order. Language constitutes one way by which the
special nature of humans shines forth. Gerhard Von Rad, the
eminent Old Testament scholar noted: "The creation of man [*sic*]
is introduced more impressively than any preceding work by the
announcement of a divine resolution: 'Let us make man.' God
participates more intimately and intensively in this than in the
earlier works of creation."[2] Besides the impressive introduction,
the clustering of the word "create" in verse 27 suggests the
creation of humans is the key focus. It suggests that when He
made humans, God reached the very apex of His creative
purpose.[3]

This attention to the creation of humans affirms our
uniqueness in the eyes of God. Furthermore, it declares that God
holds us inherently valuable. We represent more than useless
chaff, good only to be thrown to the wind. Rather, we possess
infinite worth. And so Mascall wrote: "…human nature is
something which is certified by God as inherently worth while
[sic] and, that with all its variety and flexibility, it has certain
definite characteristics which must be respected, preserved, and
developed."[4] Because He esteems us highly, God carefully
crafted a hospitable world to ensure our well-being. To honor
God, we cannot ignore our well-being. To do so dishonors the
God who created us.

Created in the Image of God

Besides this language highlighting humans as the height of
God's creation, Genesis records that God created us in His image.

This capacity to image God in the world rests uniquely with humans. Nothing else in creation images God. Certainly, God could have found other candidates in the created order. For example, the sun and the moon in their respective brilliance seem worthy of consideration. Their sheer radiance and beauty seem to make them candidates to image God. In fact, some pagan cultures have drawn this conclusion. As a result, they worship the sun, moon and stars as gods and goddesses. That's evidently not what God has in mind. God deems none of these heavenly bodies worthy to bear His image. God images Himself in the world in only one way—through humanness. Humans are the only creatures who disclose something about the reality of God.[5]

People from earlier times likely understood imaging better than we do. That's because ancient kings engaged in the practice of imaging themselves. They placed likenesses of themselves throughout their provinces as a way of representing their authority. God seems to be doing something akin to this, but in a whole different way. These ancient kings placed *fixed* representations of themselves. Their images could not speak, choose or act. God, however, has chosen humans who *can* speak, choose, act and otherwise graciously respond to their Creator's dictates. This, in some ways, images God who freely interacts with His creation. It points not to a Being who is static and who relates in stilted fashion with His creation, but rather to One who shows Himself dynamic, vibrant and interactive with His created world.

What do we mean by the image of God? Many see the image of God in humans as applying to our philosophical, psychological and theological nature. They point to our spiritual capacities, reasoning ability, intellectual talents, our capacity to rule and similar qualities. Others suggest, and I believe rightly so, that the image of God in the Genesis text refers primarily to the human capacity for *dominion*. God has endowed humankind with authority to rule and to reign on the earth. But let us understand precisely what this means. Although we possess this great authority, our dominion is not to be a dictatorship. History is replete with abuses of human power and authority. Rather, as God's stewards and representatives in this world, we are called to rule with love, graciousness and respect. And while this dominion may be the primary image in Genesis, it also foreshadows several secondary images not fully revealed in the creation narrative. In other words, dominion can be seen here as an embryonic term. It's pregnant with all sorts of possibilities of what it means to image God. These possibilities are as varied as humans themselves. We only understand this concept more fully as we move through Scripture and see how it is developed.[6]

I also agree with those who believe the *whole* person images God.[7] This understanding keeps faith with Hebrew concepts of persons. Their view was not a segmented one. Rather, they understood the person as a whole. Consequently, they would not think of the person in parts as we do. For them, the whole person likely reflected God. Of course, this understanding creates some problems. For one, it raises the question of how one's physical aspects image God. This concern is understandable. One must avoid at all costs any suggestion of ascribing corporeality to God.[8] At the same time, we ought to remember that the biblical text suggests that humans bear some semblance to the reality, but are not exact duplicates. We are like God in some ways, but we lack His fullness.[9] There is not a one-for-one correspondence. By example, when we speak about a human's physical nature, we do not imply that God is also a physical being. Our physical nature is merely the means by which we act and work. Of course, this aspect might *reflect* God as an active being. He demonstrates the capacity to reason, weigh choices and act. In addition, God possesses abilities we can only describe through our physical categories: He has a mouth to speak, ears to hear and eyes to see. None of this means He has a physical body, but simply means He possesses abilities we identify with our human frame.

However we choose to understand the image of God, one message should be abundantly clear: we reflect God in the world. This truth imparts sacredness to human life. As a result, we ought to approach and treat human persons with dignity and respect worthy of those who reflect God. We ought also to treat our entire being with the reverence and care befitting one created in God's likeness.

We Matter to God

If we stand at the apex of God's creation, if we indeed image God, what does this mean for ministers? Several implications occur to me. Being the apex of creation suggests we matter to God. He accepts us and we possess infinite value in His eyes. I am not sure we always know this. We sometimes act as though we must earn God's acceptance and define our worth by our efforts. In reality, God has already doubly accepted and affirmed us. God loves and esteems us as His creatures. Additionally, as His new creatures in Christ, He has placed His seal of approval on us. He owns us as His beloved. Such knowledge moves us beyond needing to prove who we are by what we do. Knowing ourselves as the Father's beloved helps us cope with all kinds of successes and failures without losing our identity. That's because we know our identity *before* we start ministry. We do not rely on ministry to tell us who we are. Knowing we are loved and esteemed by God frees us to minister with singleness of purpose. We minister out of love for God and humanity alone. We do not minister to establish and bolster our acceptance. On the other hand, according to Nouwen, when we do not know we are the beloved, we may spend much of our time desperately seeking approval and accolades for our personal accomplishments.[10]

Guarding Our Well-being

Because we matter to God, He created for us a healthy, hospitable environment. Evidently God was deeply concerned about our well-being. If that's true, should we care any less? Yet, judging by how we treat ourselves, it's clear we do not really value our well-being. Sometimes we act as if the callous disregard of our health actually constitutes a badge of honor. We act as if this disregard is done for the glory of God. It's not! God doesn't get any glory from attitudes and behaviors that cheapen our worth. He created us with value and doesn't intend that we treat ourselves without appropriate regard. Knowing who we are calls us to a new appreciation for and attention to our own welfare. From this perspective, managing personal well-being is a Christian's duty. Because of whose we are, we must preserve and maintain our health.

Among ministers, this responsibility often falls on deaf ears. Sometimes we ignore and abuse our health as though it doesn't matter. The consequences are usually devastating. Recently I sat in a seminar with a former superintendent of a mainline denomination. According to him, in the previous year the church conference had been in danger of exhausting its insurance limits. This unfortunate situation arose because several ministers needed medication for stress-related disorders. What's more, several gave evidence of poor health. Many struggled with weight problems. Sadly, these problems appeared most often in younger ministers in the early phases of ministry. The conference became so concerned that they instituted a new policy. Ministerial candidates who were greatly overweight and who applied to the conference would need to attend an accountability group for three years to address the problem.

We find similar problems elsewhere. For example, in 1990 the Southern Baptist Convention reported that, after maternity benefits, the largest portion of $64.2 million was paid to pastors for stress-related illness.[11] I also know of ministry groups where similar problems run rampant. In one organization, many of the ministers experience health and emotional difficulties. They show symptoms indicative of anxiety- and mood-related disorders. Cardiovascular problems like high blood pressure and heart attacks frequently appear. Astoundingly, many are in the prime of life. One does not expect to see these kinds of health problems in people so young.

In spite of these attitudes towards our bodies, we can readily find substantial evidence demanding reverence for our bodies and our health. For one, Paul reminded the Corinthians that their bodies were temples of the Holy Spirit. Caring for that temple does not simply mean avoiding evil and wickedness (1 Corinthians 6:14-7:1). It also means exerting effort to keep the temple in good shape. This means guarding our physical and emotional health. Paul reminded the Romans that their bodies were the means through which they rendered service. So he exhorted them "to offer your bodies as living sacrifices, holy and pleasing to God—this is your spiritual act of worship" (Romans 12:1). Paul understood that bodies were sacred vessels. Frances Havergal, the hymn writer who penned "Take My Life and Let it Be," also knew this truth. As part of consecration to God, she knew that hands and feet, lips and voice needed to be dedicated to God. How can one consecrate and use these organs if the body is in disrepair? As part of our consecration to God, we ought to include a commitment to our total well-being as best we can.

Forgotten Dimensions

Why do we ministers ignore these concerns? It's partly because we consider some aspects of the image more important than others. Instead of giving attention to the varied dimensions of our lives, we may respect a few and disregard others. For example, most of us agree on the need to attend our spiritual selves (whether we do is another question). We also tend to reverence our occupational selves and hold our capacity to serve in high regard. Beyond valuing these two dimensions, however, we often all but ignore our emotions, our mental and social dimensions. The truth is, we are often lousy at caring for ourselves. An Episcopal minister said it well. He noted, "We are generally workaholics, and we are great at fixing other people, but we don't have the foggiest notion of what to do for ourselves."[12]

He's right! This ignorance contributes to the abuse of our bodies, emotions, minds and relationships in the name of ministry. We work horrendous hours and never take time to allow our bodies needed refreshment. We burden ourselves with more than we can emotionally handle. As a result, we often experience symptoms like depression, anger, anxiety and burnout. We drain ourselves emotionally and finally go down in flames like a downed aircraft. We allow little time for maintaining our intellectual capacities. We lack time to read, to learn and otherwise challenge and stimulate our own minds. Even when we desire to mentally stimulate ourselves, we have so exhausted ourselves that little energy remains for such an exercise. On another front, we often have little time and energy for the significant relationships in our lives. Even when we are physically present, we may be emotionally unavailable to them. That's because we are preoccupied with other concerns—concerns deriving from our work in ministry.

The pastor quoted above rightly noted our workaholic tendencies. That's why we so readily give attention to work. In fact, we give it so much attention, it crowds out all other dimensions. If we truly understood that our whole selves image

God, we would not allow one dimension, legitimate though it is, to displace all other aspects. Not even sacred work like doing ministry would preempt the rest of our lives as it currently does.

Getting Beyond the Addiction to Ministry

Since work (doing ministry) binds us in its addictive clutches, an additional word on this subject is in order. I have often found that workaholic tendencies spring from faulty images of God. We often act as though God, like some hard taskmaster, drives us mercilessly to do more and more. We envision a deity who motivates with whips much like the slave masters of Egypt. He painfully compels us to make bricks from straw. What's more, He doesn't provide the resources for the job. We must scavenge to find our own raw materials. To use another faulty image, we often see God as a grudging boss, never satisfied with our efforts. He constantly confronts us with charges of incompetence and slacking. To prove ourselves, He demands we slavishly and constantly grind at the mill. Such images besmirch God!

Perhaps that's why God models a different picture for us. In the creation narrative, God shows that true creative activity always includes a place for rest. He evidently means we should image Him in this way as well. We should work. We should reserve time to assess and take delight in all we do. And then we should rest so we may return refreshed to new endeavors. I will say more about this in the next chapter. However, suffice it to say that the ability to rest from work is an ultimate sign of self-assurance.[13] God rested because He possessed full confidence in His ability to finish what He had begun. He exhibited no nerve-wracking doubts. Neither did He fear things falling apart unless He remained constantly active. We, on the other hand, often exhibit these traits. We think the success of our churches depends largely upon us—upon our efforts and our energy. Thus, we think we must continually be present, continually doing, in order to stop our work from falling apart.

Some time ago, I was leading a seminar for clergy. One minister, whom I will call "Jack," indicated that he needed to be in constant contact with his church. As a result, he was constantly on his cell phone, sometimes disrupting the seminar when his phone rang. Later, he confessed feelings of guilt when absent from his church. I inquired about other times when he had been absent. There weren't many. In fact, there had only been one other such occasion. The other time had been a few months earlier when had spent a few days away at another ministers' conference. Like a mother still nursing her child, Jack found it difficult to wean himself from his church. I proceeded to ask him about the condition of the church when he returned. Had the church fallen apart? Were there deep divisions splitting his congregation? Had the church members fared less well because he had left them? With a wry, knowing grin, he said they had been fine. They hardly missed him. We are not as indispensable as we think. Parishioners are not as dependent as we sometimes believe.

Sometimes we fail to realize that ultimately the work does not depend on us but on God. Walter Brueggemann, the eminent commentator is right. If we knew that truth, we could rest in confidence, not in ourselves, but in the God who upholds all things. Then we would have learned "…that life does not depend upon our feverish activity of self-securing, but that there can be a pause in which life is given to us simply as a gift."[14]

Workaholic tendencies also derive from a sense of inadequacy. As such, achievement at work often constitutes a desperate attempt to prove our worth. It often serves as a way to "pile up feel goods," and bolster our worth. At the same time, we often become addicted to work because we seek to avoid ourselves or to detract attention from some negative in our lives. The things we avoid vary. Work might help us escape from difficulties at home or from the fear of losing our jobs. It might be a way to shield ourselves from scathing criticism by church members, or to avoid the ubiquitous guilt. In other words, work addiction usually arises from the futile desire to avoid some past or present pain that beckons our attention. We hope that by keeping busy we can silence the inner voice which screams for attention. So we occupy ourselves with more and more stuff; anything to drown the cries within! So, one minister could write: "I allowed my life to become a work binge of giving, giving, giving, until I became aware of my own pain and loneliness."[15] For him, workaholic behavior in ministry represented a futile attempt to escape from pain and loneliness.

Created for Intimacy with God

God's creation of humans greatly highlights the theme of intimacy. This theme appears all across creation. It's resident in the image of God as host preparing for honored guests. But that's not all! God acts in different ways when it comes to humans. In Genesis, He announced them differently than the rest of creation. Moreover, He took a hands-on approach in creating humans. His creative activity which birthed human life was not initiated by words. Rather, God got intimately involved in this creative endeavor. He fashioned clay with tender design, suggesting a desire for direct contact with the man He was creating. The same delicate hands-on approach was evident in the creation of the woman. Both creative acts involving humans were pregnant with intimacy. God did not create people from a distance; He desired to be up close and personal. Unlike a scared father pacing the hall while his child comes into the world, God was right there in the birthing room—involved, helping, touching and birthing new life.[16]

The theme of intimacy is also visible after God created the man and the woman. God spoke directly only to humans. They alone experienced intimate relations with their Creator. It is not that God resists relating to all of His creation. According to Brueggemann, God relates to all His creation by closeness and distance. This dual theme highlights His care for creation, balanced with creation's freedom to be, to choose and act. God is close to creation and graciously attends to it. Yet He does not force or coerce His creation.[17] This dual theme applies especially to humans. They "...are honored, respected, and enjoyed by the one who calls them to be. And this gives human persons their inalienable identity."[18] They are close to God but He does not force their habits. Instead, He gives them freedom and invites them to choose those things that would lead to their greatest good.

God's intimacy with the couple continued after He created them. Like a good host, God met with them in the cool of the afternoon (Genesis 3:8). This seems to have been an accustomed activity. So it was strange when on a particular day they were not there to meet with Him. They had disobeyed and thereby broken their bond with God. Yet even in this moment of estrangement, God was still for them. He clothed them, giving them appropriate covering. What an image of intimate care! God is One who can be both tough and tender.

Getting Up-close and Personal

Evidently, God created humans for intimacy with Him. God wants us up close and personal. Such closeness to God promotes likeness to God. This is the ultimate goal of human life: to know God, to enjoy Him and to become like Him. In *The Christ of the Mount*, E. Stanley Jones highlights this truth. For him, our ultimate purpose is nothing other than godlikeness.[19] That's the primary reason for developing intimacy with God—it's intimacy for the purpose of knowing God and becoming like Him.

Failing to understand fully our critical need for intimacy with God, ministers too readily sacrifice it for other pursuits. A variety of authors demonstrate that intimacy with God often gets lost in the shuffle as clergy busily pursue the work of ministry. They pursue the activity but lose touch with the Author of all reality. In *Spiritual Wholeness for Clergy*, the authors found that the broken clergy who came to the Barnabas Center had one thing in common: loss of intimacy with God.[20] No wonder they fell. It's impossible for ministers to serve effectively without intimate connection to God.

Lack of intimacy with God deprives us of the ultimate basis for love and acceptance. We miss knowing the God who accepts us and calls us His beloved. And we also miss the possibility for real self-intimacy. Such intimacy derives from intimate contact with the Creator. Knowing Him leads to a fuller comprehension and appreciation of ourselves.[21]

But intimacy offers more. It serves as the foundation for activity in the kingdom. It's the primary basis for our usefulness in the world. Our effectiveness rises on foundations built on God, not simply because of our knowledge of Him, our skills or abilities, but primarily because of our intimate relationship *with* Him. Our intimacy with God transforms us. We learn to love people unconditionally—like God does. We begin to see people as God sees them. They are His creatures whom He has endowed with worth. No matter how encrusted and begrimed with dirt and filth, they are still His creatures. This knowledge compels us to treat all persons as worthy of love and care. Closeness to God obviates treating people as objects, using them for our selfish purposes.

In counseling circles, "depersonalization" is the term used for relating to persons callously. It's part of the burnout process. It's when we become cynical and demeaning in our attitudes towards people. In my research with ministers and perusal of other literature, I have consistently found very low levels of depersonalization among ministers. That's even true when there were extreme levels of emotional exhaustion. Apparently, ministers, male or female, are less likely to develop callous attitudes towards those they serve. This doesn't mean that it never happens. It simply means that it's less likely to occur among those who know God. They have seen people through the eyes of God and find it difficult to see them as unworthy of care. In this sense, intimacy with God inoculates against callousness toward others. Intimacy transforms us: it helps us love as God loves; it dignifies and values human life. Intimacy with God promotes intimacy with others. It can even make us more effective models for people in the pew. One pastor realized this. He confessed he needed to love God with all his heart if he was going to instill this love in them.[22] He's right! Much of what we do is modeling—leadership by example! What better trait to model for our people than a close, radical intimacy with God!

Active Servants in the World

Previously, I noted that God placed humans in the world to image Him. The term almost suggests passivity. For example, images in an art gallery just hang on the wall. If they are observed, someone has to initiate activity and choose to view the images. Others' words, decisions and actions largely dictate the pictures' power and influence. Evidently, when it comes to people, God does not intend us to be passive in the same way. He does not intend that we live passively in the world. This is partly why He allows us freedom to choose and act. Those who image Him must choose to live actively and dynamically.

That's why God's image in humans requires that we exert influence and power in the world, but not in an abusive, dominating and manipulative manner. Rather, God calls us to exercise power as He does. Walter Brueggeman indicates that this involves "the creative use of power which invites, evokes and permits."[23] We truly follow God when we choose to give permission to others, and when we use power to serve rather than dominate.

Not surprisingly, Jesus best exemplified the creative wedding of power and servanthood. He used power to serve rather than as an opportunity to attain greater power. If we want to image God's power, we must live out this tension: the use of power without the abuse of power, or grasping after more. Grasping after power means death, whereas the servant use of power promotes life and its enhancement.[24]

This understanding of power sounds strange to many an ear. Many of us equate power with domination and exercise it for personal aggrandizement and glory. Alexander the Great provides one such example of this use of power. It is said that when he had conquered the entire known world of his day, he sat down and cried because there were no more worlds to conquer. For him, power meant domination. Gordon Gekko, the main character in the movie *Wall Street*, saw power as a means to personal aggrandizement. As a result, he used his power to trample over others as he constantly recited his mantra, "Greed is good." What a radical difference from power used by Jesus! He used it to heal and help, to enhance and empower, not impoverish others.

Becoming Slaves to Created Things

Considering human dominion over creation leads me to raise another question. If God truly meant us to have dominion over created things, what consequences ensue when we become slaves to these things? I raise this question because it seems evident that we have become slaves to things, both created and man-made. We have become enslaved to gold, silver, property and other natural resources. Additionally, we have become even more enslaved to man-made things—things like houses, cars and the gadgetry that so typifies our culture. Christians, including ministers, are not immune from this bondage. Rather than controlling things, we often allow things to control us. As a result, we spend much of our time doing those activities necessary to acquire things.

The bondage to things shows itself in another way. While I applaud and use technology and gadgets which make life easier, these sometimes control us. Gadgets like car phones, beepers, pagers, telephones and e-mail dominate our lives. I recently read a newspaper article highlighting this problem. The article blamed information overload for a great deal of the stress in our current business environment. The things we hoped would make our life easier—things like e-mail and cell phones—have instead brought complications. One harried real estate and business attorney lamented that gadgets had "tethered him to work and usurped his private life." Because his legal clients insisted he contact them by e-mail, he had to check it every five minutes. Clients also expect to reach him 24-7. "It's a blow to my privacy. It doesn't just affect me at the office, its affects my life."[25]

What Adam and Eve could not achieve, technology has finally made possible. They sought to become omniscient like God. We strive for equality with God in terms of omnipresence. Technology allows us to be omni-available. But because we lack divinity, going beyond our limits devastates us. Workaholic behavior, stress, burnout and illness are but a few of the consequences derived from allowing things to control us.

Exerting Servant Leadership

How does this apply to ministry? First, it affirms our call to live as servants in the world. As servants of God we possess power. As we all know, however, power can corrupt the user. Power may become an end in itself. Power may be grasped after for our own aggrandizement and status in the world. We have seen numerous examples of ministers who used their power to line their pockets. The collapse of Heritage USA and the fall of the Bakker's supplies ample evidence of this tendency.

Ministers are not immune from the temptation to misuse power. Jesus' original disciples were not. The "Sons of Thunder" wanted to call down fire from heaven to burn up the people of Samaria because they did not receive Jesus (Luke 9:51-55). Jesus had to rebuke them. They did not seem to understand that their power was intended to bless, not harm.

Sometimes, we may see power as something to guard zealously for ourselves. So, we sometimes hesitate sharing this power with others. The Gospel of Luke provides another example of this tendency. John informed Jesus that they had found one who cast out demons in His name (Luke 9-49-50). One would think this a cause for rejoicing: others were coming on board and God's power was being felt in the kingdom of darkness. Instead, the disciples' reaction surprises us. They forbade the man from speaking in Jesus' name. It's as though this man had intruded on and exercised power meant to be consolidated in their hands alone. They misunderstood the meaning of power and its responsible use in the kingdom. Significantly, both incidents noted above occur in a context where Jesus discussed servant leadership. The whole passage is evidence that the disciples did not fully understand the nature of servant leadership.

Rather than grasping after and clinging to power, God calls us to give power to others. That's essentially what empowerment means. It involves giving power or authority to others. God provides the supreme example of empowerment. He empowered humans at creation. Then He called them to exert benevolent dominion in the world on His behalf. Similarly, we are called to give power to others rather than grasp and seek to consolidate power in our hands alone.

I can't help but wonder if this desire to consolidate power in our hands partly contributes to our reluctance to release the laity for ministry. Could it be that we fear their empowerment will translate into a loss of pastoral power? I do not mean to suggest that failure to release ministry is primarily a pastoral problem. But it is part of the problem. We would do well to be like Jesus who readily empowered the disciples for ministry. In doing so we would likely find that, rather than a diminishing of power, there would be an explosion of God's power within the life of the church.

Finally, we may grasp after power because its use can serve to carve out a position of honor and attention for us. This attitude also characterized the disciples. They sought to use their closeness to Jesus to ascend to a position of power. Thus, they wanted positions on the right hand and left hand of Jesus when He came into His kingdom. Jesus had to teach them a lesson in humbly exercising power for the benefit of others (Mark 10:35-45).

What protects ministers from the misuse and abuse of power? Only by living so close to God that we become like Him. Though possessing all power, He chose to exercise power for the benefit of creation. He also chose to partner with us by sharing His power. He calls us to image Him in His attitude and exercise of power. He calls us to give power away so that others may be changed and blessed. In the process, we will find our burdens of ministry lightened. Furthermore, we enhance our own possibility for being more human.

A final word about power and dominion may be in order. Earlier, I noted that instead of controlling things, we often allow things to control us. This certainly has some implications for ministry. A cartoon I frequently use in clergy seminars demonstrates the ministry application. In the cartoon, male and female ministers stand around a bonfire. They eagerly and joyously throw various gadgets into the raging inferno. One almost imagines them singing, "Free at last! Free at last! Thank God Almighty, I'm free at last!" Liberation has come! What are the gadgets that had bound them? The caption at the bottom gives the answer. It reads: "The Pastoral Stress Reduction Retreat solemnly concludes with the burning of beepers, car phones, and 'numbers where I can be reached.'" That's it! It was bondage to technology that allowed them to move beyond their boundaries of time. They imagined such things would truly set them free to serve. Rather, they became chained to gadgets which threatened to destroy their well-being through the temptation to live outside their God-ordained, human limits.

In order for us ministers to remain within our human limits, we must learn to control things like technology. We must refuse the temptation to be omnipresent. I recently learned a new term for persons who refuse to allow technology to dominate their lives. The term is "tech-no." Tech-nos are persons who resist the global impulse to be constantly connected. They reject the technological trend which dominates so many others. Some tech-nos reject all technology. Others are more discriminating in their choices and use only what they absolutely need.

I confess I am a tech-no. I have not rejected all technology. I use modern gadgets like computers, e-mail and PDA's. They serve useful purposes, helping me manage my work and calendar more efficiently. But against the continuing urges of a myriad of persons, I have said no to things like beepers, BlackBerry® devices and cell phones. I have made a conscious decision not to be omni-available. Though the advantages of technology are many, there are also difficulties: "The difficulty is the inability of people to disconnect. Some people become addicted to being gotten to: for most of us, it's a bit of a burden."[26]

Ministers sometimes fall victim to being omnipresent, constantly connected, constantly available. As a result they push past their human limits. They have little solitude and opportunity for contemplation. Rather, constant availability and connections sap them. So, I have said no to cell phones. To quote a fellow tech-no: "Not being available to be phoned when I am out: That is blissful."[27]

1. E. L. Mascall, *The Importance of Being Human* (New York: Columbia University Press, 1958), p. 32.
2. Gerhard Von Rad, *Genesis* (Philadelphia: The Westminster Press, 1972), p. 57.
3. Ibid., p. 57. See also Walter Brueggemann, *Genesis* (Atlanta: John Knox Press, 1982), p. 31.
4. Mascall, *The Importance of Being Human*. p. 24.
5. Brueggemann, *Genesis*, p. 32
6. I am indebted to Drs. Joe Dongell and David Thompson for their observations on the image of God in Genesis.
7. Gordon J. Wenham, *Genesis 1-15* (Waco, TX: Word Books, 1987).
8. H. C. Leopold, *Exposition of Genesis* (Grand Rapids, MI: Baker Book House, 1982).
9. George H. Livingston, *Genesis* (Kansas City: Beacon Hill Press, 1969).
10. Henri Nouwen, "Moving from solitude to community to ministry," *Leadership* 16:2 (Spring 1995): pp. 81-87.
11. Hank Whittemore, "Ministers under Stress," *Parade Magazine*, April 14, 1991, p. 4.
12. Ibid., p. 5.
13. Brueggemann, *Genesis*, p. 35
14. Ibid.
15. Whittemore, "Ministers Under Stress," p. 4.
16. Brueggeman, *Genesis*, p. 31
17. Ibid., p. 28
18. Ibid., p. 31.
19. E. Stanley Jones, *The Christ of the Mount* (Nashville, TN: Abingdon, 1981).

20. Donald Hands and Wayne L. Fehr, *Spiritual Wholeness for Clergy: A New Psychology of Intimacy with God, Self and Others* (Washington, D.C.: Alban Institute, 1993), p. 54.
21. Ibid., p. 31
22. Kevin Bidwell, "A stronger heart for worship," *Leadership* 21:2 (Spring 2000): pp. 113-115.
23. Brueggemann, *Genesis*, p. 32
24. Ibid., p. 34.
25. Carol Hymowitz and Rachel E. Silverman, "Economy, loss of control blamed for stress on job," *Business Monday, Lexington Herald Leader*, January 22, 2001, p. 9.
26. Janet Kornblum, "Meet the 'Tech-nos,' people who reject plugging into the highly wired world," *USA Today*, January 11, 2007, p. 2A.
27. Ibid.

Chapter 7

Principles for Creative Activity

Creation tutors us in varied truths about humanity. It also instructs us in sound, fundamental principles underlying creative activity. These principles are timeless. They hark back to the Creator Himself. As we investigate anew the origins of life in Genesis, we can imbibe from God Himself the nature and process of true creative activity. Drinking from His fountain of wisdom, we have an opportunity to find refreshment in ministry instead of the continual drain and dryness many experience. With these God-modeled principles in hand, we also find a basis for reframing ministry that enhances our well-being. At the same time, we will discover that this reframe does no harm to our creativity and productivity.

In this chapter I have chosen to discuss four principles of creative activity, although one could discuss others or express them differently. This is not surprising. God's truth is so rich and multifaceted it demands multiple frames. Even then, these varied frames do little justice to all the truth of God. I have chosen to discuss the following principles and how they might serve to help us reframe ministry:

1. The power of speech.
2. Boundaries which bring order from chaos.
3. Balance and rhythm in the creative process.
4. Rest as an essential part of creativity.

The Creative Power of Speech

Genesis gives a prominent role to speech in creative endeavors. God's speech conveyed His power. His speech created and caused things to live which did not exist previously. This is part of the emphasis in the Genesis creation narrative. Everything, except humanity, was created by the sheer power of God's creative word. "Let there be light!" And light came forth in radiant splendor. Each creative day began with a similar command: "Let there be...," and it was so. So light and sky, sea and land, birds, fish and animals came forth commanded by the power of His word. God spoke into being new life in varied forms. Walter Brueggemann has noted that God's characteristic action is to speak. It is through this medium that God maintains relationship with His world. For Brueggemann, "The way of God with his world is the way of language."[1] In the creation narrative, He exhibits this characteristic as He employs words to fashion and command creation, and to call humans to responsible dominion.

The Power of Speech in the Ministry of Jesus

Jesus continued His Father's same relation with the world through speech. Like His Father, He spoke to the howling wind and the battering waves, and they instantly obeyed. "The men were amazed and asked, 'What kind of man is this? Even the winds and the waves obey him!'" (Matthew 8:27 NIV). This passage demonstrates the amazement of His disciples. What manner of a man is He? Nothing more than His Father's Son! He, like His Father, commands creation and upholds it all by the word of His power. This same power of words reached even into the spirit world. As a result, time and time again, Jesus spoke to demons and they instantly responded to His words. He held such great power over them, they cringed at His feet. They needed His word of permission to do their next deed. So, in the deliverance of the demoniac at Gedara, the legions had to beg His consent to enter the swine (Mark 5:12-13).

Of course, Jesus most often spoke to people. And what power His words conveyed! He spoke to people going about their daily routine and commanded them to follow Him. He saw Simon and Andrew casting nets into the sea, commanded them to follow Him and they left their very livelihood in response. Likewise, He saw James and John mending nets. He commanded them and they immediately left the nets and their father to follow (Mark 1:16-21). What most amazes me is His power to command a man like Levi. After all, Levi plied a most dishonorable trade. His trade involved extortion and squeezing "blood" from unfortunate folk. Surely such a fellow would be too hardened, too tied to his ill-gotten gain to leave all and follow Jesus! But his response was the same as the others. He immediately left everything to follow Jesus (Mark 2:13-14). I have always been amazed by these responses. Why would these men have responded so readily to Jesus, a person they did not know?

On second thought, I should not be so amazed. Jesus has been speaking and commanding human allegiance for over two thousand years. For Him, many were willing to face the wrath of Roman emperors and the terror of their hideous tortures. But much more compelling for me is my own journey. More than thirty years ago, I, too, heard His call and followed. I left my secular ambitions, my family and my country to follow Him. Over the years I have met countless others with similar stories who left all to follow Jesus. His words command allegiance and obedience.

Jesus also demonstrated the power of speech in His teaching. His teachings rang with authority commanding attention and amazement. Even those who desired to resist His power and His way fell under the power of His words. Even if they did not obey, they expressed amazement at the power revealed in His words. A characteristic saying about the teachings of Jesus was that He taught with authority unlike the Scribes and Pharisees (Matthew 7:29). Through His teachings, Jesus brought life and healing to troubled souls. Moreover, He used words to instruct and equip those whom He called to follow Him.

Jesus gave this same power of words to His disciples. He gave His disciples the power to command nature if they had enough faith. At one point, He told His disciples that if they had faith, they could speak to mountains and have them move into the sea (Matthew 7:20). He also gave them power to command demons. To them was given the ability to heal and, in other creative ways, effect change in people's lives. Thus, after Jesus had sent them out through the villages, they came back reporting what they had done. They had preached repentance, cast out demons and healed the sick—all in the power of His name (Mark 6:12-13, 30).

Power to Hurt or to Heal

Evidently words possess great power both to hurt and heal. Concerning the power of words one playwright observed: "I really do inhabit a system in which words are capable of shaking the entire structure of government, where words can prove mightier than ten military divisions."² That's true! Hitler's *Mein Kampf* demonstrated the destructive power of words. Generally thought of as one of the most influential books ever written, it promoted the obliteration of an entire race. Misguided words can do irreparable damage.

On the other hand, clinical practices like psychotherapy constantly demonstrate the power of words to bring healing. Words can even heal those who have experienced horrific trauma. Sometimes those words may be accidentally, or unintentionally therapeutic. Once spoken, their power to heal is released. Author Raymond Corsini tells an amazing story. He had been working as a psychologist at Auburn prison in New York. One day a 30-year-old inmate came to see him. He told Dr. Corsini he would soon leave on parole. Before he left, he wanted to thank him for what he had done. Then he proceeded to tell of an event which had occurred two years earlier. Two years before, he had left Corsini's office as if walking on air. The world looked like a whole different place on that day. He felt like he had been reborn. The change wasn't simply a matter of emotion or perspective. Its roots had gone deep enough so that he actually began to act differently. Instead of hanging out with rough, seedy characters, he found more savory company. He took a job in the machine shop and learned a trade. He started going to the prison high school and obtained his diploma. In addition, he took a correspondence course in drafting and now had lined up a job in the field. As if these changes were not enough, he started attending church and reconnected with his parents. He summed it all up by saying, "I now have hope. I know who and what I am. I know I will succeed in life. I plan to go to college. You have freed me. I used to think you bug doctors…were for the birds, but now I know better. Thanks for changing my life."³

Corsini sat amazed as he listened to the story. There was just one problem. He couldn't remember speaking to the young man. Finally, he looked at his folder and could find nothing more than a note about having given the young man an IQ test. Still puzzled, Corsini wondered if it was a case of mistaken identity. Had this young man confused him with someone else? The young man was adamant. It was Corsini. What forgotten miracle had Corsini worked which transformed this inmate? The young man briefly replied, "You told me I had a high IQ." That was all! *"You have a high IQ!"* These five words had radically transformed this young man's life. Never underestimate the power of words, even human words, to transform lives!

Recapturing the Power of Speech

If words, even those unaided by God, possess such an ability, what must be the power of words infused by the Spirit and wielded by a man or woman who has trusted in Jesus? Simply awesome! This is the awesome power we wield when we minister in His name. Sometime ago, I read an article by William Willimon, then Dean of the Chapel at Duke Divinity School. The article, "The Power of Mere Words," demonstrated the tremendous influence words can generate. Willimon declared that words create worlds and change people in unpredictable ways because of the power of the Holy Spirit. And we can never predict how the Spirit will use our words to heal and change lives.[4] But He *does* change lives. Therefore, we can rest in the fact that we speak in His name. We can take comfort even when we, like Paul, consider ourselves unaccomplished speakers. Even then our words come in the power of the Spirit (I Corinthians 2:1-5). We can rest, watch and let Him surprise us by the miraculous changes He produces through our words.

God has called us to wield this power of words in our ministry. Indeed, communication lies at the heart of ministry. The disciples obviously understood this mandate to speak in His name. As a result, they were reluctant to leave the Word of God to serve tables. It's not that serving poor widows wasn't important. But their primary mandate was to pray and speak the Word of God to people. Others needed to provide for everyday needs. They needed to speak and invite change in the lives of people. At the same time, they needed to allow persons the freedom to be and choose rather than try to manipulate and coerce people through their speech. Words were the apostles' primary business, and it is likewise ours.

Perhaps we have lost the sense of the primacy of speech in ministry. Because of this, we often try to outfit ourselves with a myriad of skills: administration, management, human resource management, building maintenance and the like. This doesn't mean these are unimportant or unnecessary. But sometimes we forsake the Word of God to serve at other tables even when congregants are more gifted in these areas. In the process, we pay scant attention to the power of our speech to influence and equip others. We forget ministry is not about constant activity or the accumulation and use of multiple skills. It's fundamentally about speaking in God's name, through preaching, spiritual direction and other ways through which we equip the body of Christ.

Perhaps we minimize the power of speech because we do not trust our skills as preachers. We think our speech needs the façade of polished oratory to influence other people's lives meaningfully. God does use polished oratory, but He can influence and change lives simply by the power of His Spirit. The Spirit can wield even feeble words with uncanny, unpredictable and unimaginable power. Paul knew this. His speech, though not laced with flowery eloquence, clearly demonstrated the power of the Spirit (1 Corinthians 2:1-5).

Does the emphasis on the Spirit's power render effective communication and honed preaching skills unimportant? Of course not! We need to take every opportunity to enhance our skills. But even when we have done all we can to communicate effectively, we need to remember one thing: in the kingdom, effectiveness is not simply a matter of eloquence. It's about the power of the Spirit who wields our words like sharp axes— piercing and dividing wherever and however He wills.

The power of words does not show itself only *while* we speak. Their power transcends mere moments of time. Our words continue to exert power and influence long *after* we have spoken. This is because the Holy Spirit carries our words from the present into the future. He then uses them to probe and pierce even into dark places we could never imagine. Long after our voices have gone silent, the Spirit still wields our words with uncanny power and influence to re-create and enhance lives.

This ought to provoke trust and the confidence to rest. We can trust Him to produce the increase and to make our words the media for bringing influence, healing and life. We can trust Him even when we think our words lacked something; even when we do not think we communicated as effectively as we desired. Having spoken in His name, we can rest in confidence. We rest in the knowledge He still works, still uses our words and our work. This knowledge alone might save many a preacher from the many self-recriminations which burden us once we leave the pulpit.

Boundaries: From Chaos to Order
Boundaries of Space

One should not ignore the role of boundaries in the creation narrative. Verse 1 of Genesis announces the creation of the heavens and the earth. Verse 2 tells us about one part of the created order—the earth. From this verse, we learn that it remained formless and void, unfit for human habitation. How did God bring order into this disordered and disarrayed world? He brought order through the creation of boundaries. The language of boundaries appears throughout the creation narrative. It shows itself in words like "separate," "gather" and "after its kind." At least one of these words occurs in each of the creative days. For example, God *separated* light from darkness and sea from atmosphere. He *gathered* waters together and dry land together. He called forth vegetation *after its kind* (Genesis 1:1-13). These words all connote that God was building boundaries around His created structures.

Boundaries of Time

There's also ample evidence for boundaries of *time*. In fact, God's first act involved separating light from darkness. On the fourth day, he created the sun, the moon and the stars, essentially setting the stage for time as we know it. Additionally, the role of time appears prominent in the consistent phrase occurring throughout the narrative: "And there was evening and morning." These word and acts highlight limits placed around time. One might argue about the length of time involved, but God clearly ordered His world with evident respect for the limits of time. He bounded the daylight by the darkness of night. He limited the night by bringing forth streaming rays of sunlight which ushered in the dawn. Day and night each had their limits—"there was evening and morning." This has always been God's master plan. The day of activity or the night of rest should not dominate our lives. Both must have their place.

Boundaries in Relationships

In addition, God's provision of boundaries transcends time and space. God provided rules governing how creation members should relate to each other and their newly formed world. Over the last three creative days, which largely involve populating the earth, we find similar language denoting boundaries. Much of the emphasis in these creative days focuses on creating *after one's kind*. This makes sense because God intended boundaries around the various species. As a result, he created each species of animal with definitive boundaries, forbidding it to cross over to other species. They could relate to each other, but not in the intimate ways possible within species. Also, Adam's language about Eve being his bone and his flesh might point to a boundary around human relationships. Adam's language may be another way to say, "She is of my kind." Thus, we also find a boundary of intimacy around the couple into which no other creature, human or animal, must intrude.

Furthermore, Adam and Eve must relate to creation in a certain way. They must superintend the garden and have dominion over the world. We have already noted elsewhere that their dominion over creation meant servant leadership and stewarding of creation. Yet God did not give them *carte blanche*. God set a limit on how they should function in the world: they should not eat of the one tree in the garden. Were they free? Undoubtedly. But true freedom always involves loving limits. This is evident here. If they lived within these limits, they would do well. If they violated these boundaries, they could expect turmoil and devastation.

Boundaries around Activity and Energy

Permit me to highlight a couple more boundaries. Their importance became evident to me through a student in a doctor of ministry course on stress. I had begun the class with the Genesis creation narrative. After I stopped the tape, I asked the class for their thoughts about the passage. Almost immediately, one pastor asked, "This is God who is creating, right?" I readily agreed and he immediately continued: "Well, why does He take so much time to get the job done? If this was me, I would have done it in one day." I suspect many pastors feel the same way. We sometimes tire of God who seems to be dilly-dallying. Why doesn't He just get on with it? But God leisurely takes His time. He almost seems like the stereotypic southerner trying to calm a hasty young man: "Son, some things just take time. You can't rush creativity."

To what boundaries does this point? Two readily come to mind, and both are related. First, it involves boundaries around our *activities*. How much will we try to accomplish during a given time period? Will we cram our plates with more than we can humanly handle, or will we set a reasonable limit to how much we attempt? Even though God evidently could have done it all in a day, He doesn't—"Some things just take time."

Second, at the risk of overextending the image, I suggest it also highlights the *need to conserve energy and personal resources* in creative activity. I do not suggest God gets tired and needs rest. Rather, I propose He models for us how we should function and conserve our energy. We cannot always be at it. We need to take breaks in between our work, allowing pause to assess and to permit our creative juices to flow. God himself does this. He does not rush madly about or exhibit furious activity. Rather, He shows himself a master craftsman deliberately going about his trade. There are no wasted movements, no aimless energy, just calm, deliberate creativity. When He's finished with the day's tasks, He surveys the results. Satisfied with a job well done, He pauses until another day. If only we would take the same approach in our activities and learn how to set boundaries around our energy and our activity!

Healthy Relating through Boundaries

I suspect the language of boundaries inspires Brueggemann's emphasis on closeness and distance in the creation narrative. Another way of saying closeness and distance is to speak of gathering and separateness. Belonging and separateness constitute familiar themes in family therapy circles. They are concepts inherent to boundaries and permit healthy relating. Too much belongingness or closeness leads to fusion and enmeshment in which persons cannot be distinguished from each other. One family therapist called families characterized by unhealthy boundaries "the undifferentiated family ego mass."[5]

That's a family of confused relationships where everyone thinks, feels and acts alike. There's no distinctness, no individual sense of personhood and no freedom to respond as one chooses. On the other hand, one can have too much distance (separateness). In such cases, members are not able to relate to each other and may cut themselves off totally. Healthy relationships always involve a good blend of separateness and closeness—in other words, good boundaries.

This is evidently what God intends. He created a world in which the parts were meant to relate to each other. But He did not create the parts as clones of each other. Each created thing has its own role and distinctness in the world. To confuse parts would only invite chaos. To avoid chaotic disarray, God deeply imbedded into all of nature the law of boundaries. When we faithfully observe these boundaries, we do well. When we foolishly ignore them, we plunge ourselves into chaos and conflict. This rule applies to all of life and relationships. It applies to how we relate to limits of space, time, relationships and energy. It relates to our connection with the earth and created things. And yes, it even applies to how we separate our personal identity from our occupation and activities.

Perhaps this is why so many people are talking boundaries. In many circles, secular and sacred, people are talking about the need for boundaries. A few years ago, John Townsend and Henry Cloud wrote their immensely popular book, *Boundaries*. On many Christian campuses and in many churches, groups are getting into this popular topic. Some have reacted to what they see as the church capitulating to social science.

A few summers ago, I presented a seminar on boundaries. In the audience was a seminary student. I did not start the presentation with the concept of boundaries. I started with the Genesis creation narrative. After it was all over, this student approached me. He told me he avoided these types of seminars because he could not find any biblical bases for talking about boundaries. For him, talk about boundaries represented another way in which the church sacrificed the Bible for psychological jargon. Now he had changed his mind. He had found a biblical basis for building boundaries into his own life.

Encouraging boundaries is a fundamental biblical principle, not just a social science thing. It's built by God himself into the fabric of the universe to prevent His creation from falling into chaotic disarray. One does not have to look far to find the truth and wisdom of this law. I guarantee that wherever one finds a person who eschews appropriate boundaries, one will find a chaotic life in constant turmoil and pain. On the other hand, wherever one finds healthy boundaries, one will find a rich, tranquil and productive life.

Building Boundaries in Ministry

The notion of boundaries evidently applies to ministry. Ministers possess a notorious reputation for not setting boundaries in their lives. It's a reputation justly earned. Because we do not set boundaries in our lives, we often overfunction for others. Mark's pastor provided a powerful example of this. You see, Mark had become more than a parishioner; he was more like a brother and friend. Ignoring boundary issues, he moved Mark into his home with his wife and teenage daughter. But Mark had a major problem—he was addicted to drugs. A multiplicity of problems accompanied his addiction: anger, acting out, relapse and self-damaging behavior. These behaviors threatened to engulf the pastor and his family in a destructive downward spiral. One day he spent many hours searching for Mark in the town's bars. When he finally found him, Mark wouldn't talk to him. In a desperate attempt to influence Mark, he wound up riding the hood of Mark's car, clinging to the wipers, trying to reason with him through the glass as Mark sped away. This is an excellent example of a lack of boundaries and overfunctioning behavior. Not surprisingly, these problems created increasing problems in the pastor's life, family and ministry. He needed Mark apparently a whole lot more than Mark needed him. Thus he wrote:

> My needing Mark caused problems in my pastoral ministry. I became so obsessed, so numbed with pain over Mark, that I wasn't good for anything or anyone else. I'd grope through each day in a sort of daze, unable to focus, unable to give myself to those who needed me. My study time deteriorated and I hadn't

the energy for even routine administrative duties. I was a basket case at home, unable to provide emotion-ally [*sic*] for my family. [6]

Thankfully, he found his way out of this disabling entanglement.

Sometimes ministering without appropriate boundaries provokes far more serious consequences. One such consequence involves incidents where ministers become sexually involved with parishioners. Confusion, turmoil and chaos often ensue, not only for the minister but also for their family, for the church and the community. It's dangerous to minister and live without boundaries. Genesis teaches us that boundaries provide the opportunity to move from chaos to ordered living.

Ministers need to set boundaries around their space. This includes how much they allow other people to intrude on their need for space and distance. One prominent need involves creating boundaries around the parsonage and parsonage life. The parsonage ought to be the private space of the minister regulated by the parsonage family and not the church committee.

Ministers desperately need to set boundaries around their time. Time problems consistently rank as a top stressor for ministers. Rather than having too much time, many ministers have too little. One 1991 study by the Fuller Institute of Church Growth showed that over 90% of ministers worked more than 46 hours per week.[7] I wonder if that number included the countless late-night meetings and calls ministers receive. As a result, many ministers have inadequate time for their families. It's not surprising that in 1992, a *Leadership* article related that 81% of pastoral couples felt that they had insufficient time together.[8] In fact, this problem was at the top of the list. By not setting boundaries with others, pastors had little time left to nurture and foster healthy relationships at home.

Closely related to this is the need to set boundaries around the time given to activities and around their energies. Ministers need to limit the amount of time they stay at a task. Sometimes they need to understand some tasks can remain undone. This is especially true when people do not see the need for the task or program in the first place. In such cases the task survives—

barely—only by the efforts of the minister. Additionally, ministers need to limit the number of activities they attempt. Too many of us try to juggle too many balls with little success. We cannot do everything.

Doubtless, the lack of boundaries around time and activities has devastating consequences. No wonder many pastors struggle with their physical, mental and emotional energies! They are depleted in these areas because they have invested too much of themselves without finding opportunities for replenishment. It's a recipe for burnout. To give ourselves to far too many people over long periods of time can only ensure our complete exhaustion.

Ministers also need another vital boundary: to separate their identity from their occupation. Among professionals, ministers especially tend to lose themselves in their roles. They often become enmeshed in ministry to the point of losing their sense of personal identity. Part of the problem may spring from the source of their calling. Because God called them to ministry, they may believe this justifies losing themselves in their role. They must certainly serve faithfully to this high calling. However, this never means losing oneself. God intends for ministers to stay keenly aware of their identity and humanity while doing ministry. The two are not the same. Ministry is not who we are, it's what we do.

Finding Balance and Rhythm

I have already implied a rhythm and balance to creation. Biblical commentators have consistently pointed to how creation proceeds with symmetry and moves in an orderly sequence. One can catch this by simply looking at the structure of the creative days. Consider the following:

Day 1 – Creation of light

Day 2 – Separation of sea and sky

Day 3 – Creation of dry land, etc.

Day 4 – Creation of lesser luminaries

Day 5 – Creation of sky and water animals

Day 6 – Creation of land animals[9]

One cannot fail to see the balance and rhythm in God's activity. His first three days lay out the space. He moves like an artist carefully laying out the canvas upon which he will subsequently lavish his masterful brush strokes. The second three days largely serve to populate the space He has created. In the whole narrative, God proceeds with a design and purpose which betray a hidden, lavish, though still unrevealed, master plan,. Nothing He does smacks of randomness or haphazardness. Everything maintains a delicate, deliberate balance. Light must give rise to lesser lights. Sea and sky must find inhabitants to play across their vast expanses. Land must have animals roaming its terrain and the patter of human feet. Nothing is left to chance. Nothing is left out of kilter.

We also see this symmetry in another aspect prominent in the text. Brueggemann has noted this symmetry and careful sequence in the following way:

> Command: "God said, Let there be…"
> Execution: "And it was so."
> Assessment: "God saw that it was good."
> Time: "there was evening and morning…"[10]

Each creative day except day two has this sequence. Day two lacks the formula of approbation—"God saw that it was good." Everything else is in place throughout the narrative. When God had created humans and given them their charge, we find another variation of God's assessment. He pronounced His finished work "very good" (Genesis 1:31). It suggests to me a painter finishing his work with a final, delicate stroke from his brush and standing back to gaze in approval. He knows he has just created a masterpiece.

Who can miss the other inherent evidences of balance in God's creative activity? Who can miss the overt balance between rest and activity? The evening of rest must give rise to a new dawn of activity. All this strikes me as poetry in motion. The balancing of the first three days with the last three days seems to me like poetic meter measured out in light and darkness, sky and sea, inanimate objects and living things. Each creative day stands like a poetic stanza, complete in itself, a thing of wonder and beauty to behold, yet awaiting other stanzas to make the poem a finished work of art.

Not surprising, I have found this balance and rhythm most beautifully rendered in a poem. This poem is also a prayer of thanksgiving. J. Philip Newell captures it in *Celtic Benediction*. Significantly, it comes from the Saturday morning prayer—the day of rest in the creation narrative.

> For the night followed by the day
> for the idle winter ground
> followed by the energy of spring
> for the infolding of the earth
> followed by bursts of unfolding
> thanks be to you, O God.
> For rest and wakefulness
> stillness and creativity
> reflection and action
> thanks be to you.
> Let me know in my own body and soul
> the rhythms of creativity that you have established.
> Let me know in my family and friendships
> the disciplines of withdrawal and the call to
>   engagement.
> Let me know for my world
> the cycles of renewal
> given by you for healing and health
> the pattern of the seasons
> given by you for the birth of new life.[11]

The author of this prayer beautifully captures the balance and rhythm of creation: night followed by day, winter followed by spring, the infolding and outfolding of the earth. The created world sings in tune and rhythm to the music of God. But not just creation! Humans must also find in their lives the balance imbedded by God. So the author speaks of the symmetry which must characterize humans and their activity. He speaks of rest and wakefulness, stillness and creativity, reflection and action, withdrawal and engagement. What's the purpose of it all? To bring renewal, healing and health that engenders new life.

But there's more to creation. There's deliberate, yet unhurried productivity. God even takes time to survey, assess and take pleasure in what He is creating. He's not so absorbed by the end product that He cannot take moment by moment pleasure in the progress of His grand design. This seems characteristic of God's activity throughout the narrative. He takes a kind of holy pleasure and enjoyment in all He does.

In *Celebration of Discipline*, Richard Foster describes a concept he calls *otium sanctum*, or "holy leisure." It "…refers to a sense of balance in the life, an ability to be at peace through the activities of the day, an ability to rest and take time to enjoy beauty, an ability to pace ourselves."[12] I see holy leisure in creation. It springs from its ultimate source—the God of all creation. I see God exhibiting great balance both in His work and in His approach to His tasks. Throughout the whole narrative, one has the constant sense of an unhurried peace—"Some things just take time." God takes time to pace Himself, even though He does not need to. He evidently finds opportunities for rest punctuated by a final rest on the seventh day. And He takes time to enjoy the beauty and goodness of all He's creating. That's holy leisure, right from its source.

Significantly, researchers agree with the balanced approach to life seen in Genesis. According to the Grubb Theory of Oscillation developed at the Grubb Institute in London, everyone needs to oscillate between varied modes of life if they want to do well. The theory suggests several poles between which persons must move. For example, people must move between *being* and *doing*. That is, they must move between accepting themselves for who they are and meeting the constant demands of an achievement-oriented culture. Closely related to these two poles are the poles of *play* and *work*. Individuals must learn not only to expend their energy towards accomplishing tasks, they must also learn how to use some of that energy in play. Humans must also learn how to differentiate their *essence* from their *role* and find a place for both in their lives.[13]

What happens if one doesn't oscillate between these poles? In these cases, people tend to lose the necessary balance and become stuck on one side of the ledger. In the process, they lose touch with reality. The only way to avoid this imbalance is to find a rhythmic movement between the varied poles of life. One has to find repeated opportunities to move in a different realm. Such movement permits regaining perspective and moving back into the other mode with renewed energy and vision. For example, when a minister makes space for being instead of constant doing, it allows returning to the pastoral role with renewed gusto.

Getting Rhythm into Ministry

Clergy certainly need to find a place for balance and rhythm in ministry. We see that rhythm and balance in creation. We also see it in the life and ministry of Jesus. His ministry involved "the rhythm of public ministry and private time."[14] Shawchuck and Heuser indicate that Jesus showed an approach to life and ministry which created space for solitude and community. He constantly balanced rest and retreat with activity, withdrawal with engagement. To use Richard's Foster's term, Jesus' ministry demonstrated holy leisure. We are called to develop this same approach to life and ministry.

This truth is most evident in Mark 6:31-45. In this passage, Jesus called the disciples aside to rest from their ministry labors. He thought it was important for His tired disciples to step aside and refresh themselves. He did not mean for the disciples to serve out of tiredness and exhaustion. He wanted them fresh and alive for ministry. To achieve this, they needed to step back from the press of ministry to refresh and replenish their resources. This command to come aside shows Jesus' balanced approach to life and ministry. He demonstrates that ministry is best done in at least two movements: first, stepping aside into solitude; and second, returning refreshed to community and ministry.

The same truth applies to all aspects of the minister's life. Ministers are always more than their role. We are living, breathing human persons with the need for sustenance and relaxation amidst our activities. We need to live out a balanced approach in every area of our lives. And yet how little do we see this! Instead, we often see ministers stuck on one side of the ledger. We constantly seem to give attention to doing—to work and fulfilling our clergy roles. In the process, we often ignore being—play and our essential nature as finite creatures. Our lives often demonstrate that we are grossly out of balance. We sometimes come to believe this abnormal imbalance constitutes the normal mode for ministers.

I often use a *Doonesbury* cartoon in clergy seminars. In it, Bernie, the boss of a computer company, comes to the office only to find all the lights on in the building at midnight. As he enters, he finds several persons "spending the night crashing deadlines." He then gives them a wonderful speech about the dangers of tiring themselves out: *"No product launch is worth that kind of sacrifice. Highly stressed, chronically fatigued employees cannot give their best and I need your best"* [italics mine]. As a gracious, caring boss he continued: *"From now on I am having the power shut off in the building at 5:00 p.m. I want you to go home, lead lives, rest. We cannot build a future by trashing the present"* [italics mine].[15]

Can you imagine God saying the same thing to ministers? I can! This is the ultimate message from creation to all humanity. Unfortunately, the message often falls on deaf ears. We find a similar deaf response in the *Doonesbury* cartoon. Kim, normally very levelheaded, is the first to spout folly: "He's gone mad," she laments. Her boss has just called her to care for herself and get a life. She calls him mad. I want to ask, "Who is really the mad one?" It's Kim and all the others like her. She's worked this way for so long that sound wisdom seems like the height of foolishness. The abnormal had become normal for her. And so it does for many a minister. We become so accustomed to living on the activity side of the ledger, it eventually becomes the norm. As a result, we often fail to listen to the Jethros in our lives who call us away from folly and endless activity. We see them as unwise, maybe even unspiritual, because they call us away from ministry. In reality, we are the mad ones. We have not listened to creation and the several voices which call us to balance.

Rest which Refreshes and Restores

Among the many other themes we may explore within the creation narrative, permit me to discuss one more of these: the theme of rest. This idea reverberates throughout the whole narrative. Early on, rest seems largely implied. We see it implied when God steps back to survey and assess His ongoing work. It's like a creative pause in the midst of one's activity. The pause may not seem long, but it can work wonders. It involves a break from doing, from continually producing. That break, spurred by finding joy in what is produced, can itself provide internal motivation.

Rest, in the sense of cessation of activity, also seems apparent in the recurring phrase, "there was evening and there was morning." It occurs after each phase of the creative process. Thus, it connotes to me some sort of break from the tasks of that day.

Short breaks to rest from one's work have their own unique benefits. We have long known that employees cannot continue working non-stop. I do not speak only of lunch breaks. I speak of the fifteen-minute breaks generally allowed for every four hours of work. This largely involves a cessation of one's activity. We have now gone further. Occupational experts now advocate the value of short periods of time for actual *sleep*, not simply for cessation from work. Progressive companies across America now encourage employees to take short naps throughout their workday. They find that such periods of rest actual enhance productivity rather than hamper it. This may seem like a new discovery, but it's not! We find fundamental principles for rest amidst the activity at creation.

More definitive and explicit is the rest which comes at the end of the creation narrative (Genesis 2:1-3). One might consider the rests mentioned earlier like commas in a sentence. Using the same imagery, this final rest is more like a full stop which calls for a longer retreat from activity. That is the essence of this rest. More than a comma, it's a *period* signaling a weekly cessation from work. And it's a pause, not for worship, but for rest. Indeed, according to Walter Brueggeman, the original Sabbath in Israel revolved around rest, not worship.[16]

It's not that worship is unimportant. It's central to our lives. But people also need time simply to rest from their labor and be re-created. Eugene Peterson, author of *The Message*, makes a similar assessment. He notes that Old Testament emphases on Sabbath fall into two categories: Sabbath rest intended for prayer (worship); and a Sabbath intended for play. Thus, besides prayer and worship, Peterson notes his own opportunities for play. He describes how he often takes Sunday afternoons to go to the mountains with his wife to watch birds.[17] Evidently, bird watching constitutes play for Dr. Peterson and allows him to be refreshed and restored. That's the emphasis here—rest allowing re-creation. God's rest sets a pattern for us to follow, and reminds us that life does not depend on our constant activity. Rather, life is a gift we receive from God, separate from our strivings.[18]

Ultimately, taking time to rest demonstrates confidence in God. God rested because He was confident in His capacities. He did not fear the unraveling of His efforts if He rested. Similarly, when we rest, we demonstrate confidence in a God who works behind the scenes in all that we do. When we rest, He still works. Thus, for Walter Brueggemann, "The Sabbath is a kerygmatic *statement about the world*. It announces that the world is safely in God's hands. The world will not disintegrate if we stop our efforts. The world relies on God's promises and not on our efforts. The observance of Sabbath rest is a break with our efforts to achieve, to secure ourselves, and to make the world into our image according to our purposes."[19]

A few affirmations of confidence shine through in this quote. First, it affirms the providence of a caring God who has not left the world to struggle on its own. Rather, God abides in our midst, even though unseen. Second, it affirms that the world is not ours but God's. Many look to John Wesley and, like him, affirm the world as our parish. This is only true in one sense: God has called us to serve in the whole world. But this is where our responsibility ends. We do not uphold anything. God does. God calls us to put forth effort, but ultimately it is He who gives the increase. We are not indispensable—the life of the world does not depend on us alone. It ultimately depends on God. In fact, it's not simply the world, but everything in it which depends on God.

What a liberating word! We partner with God, but the partnership does not depend on our efforts alone. As a result, when we have faithfully done all He has called us to do, we can rest in confidence that He is still working. This kind of knowledge helps us to rest securely and peacefully. The world and our work are in His hands. With this understanding, we can break free of our efforts for achievement and security. We do not need to achieve simply to bolster ourselves physically and emotionally. We depend on God. We depend on Him for all we need and for our security. This knowledge frees us in our work. Our work becomes an opportunity to make real in the world the image of God, not to make the world like us.

Ultimately, as we build rest into our lives, we discover another truth. Rest is not a shallow interest denoting laziness. It's not a matter of avoiding achievement. Rather, rest exists for our well-being. It also better prepares us for the role which David Benner calls "soul hosts." For Benner, humans are soul hosts who "…prepare for their gift of hospitality by cultivating a place of quiet within themselves." It is also the place to which they call others to rest.[20] Although this idea of soul hosts is relevant to all Christians, it is particularly important for pastors. As pastors, we need to see rest as a substantial endeavor which involves valuing ourselves and guarding our well-being. It means shepherding our human resources as valuable treasures given by the hand of God. Therefore, to despise rest means despising both the Giver and His gift.

I have come to see rest as a fundamental part of any creative activity. Many of us likely equate creativity with activity. This is not the picture in Genesis. In fact, one could argue from the text that God's final creative act was rest. Creation did not really end until God rested. As a result, I have come to believe that true creativity is not action alone. We err whenever we identify creativity with feverish activity. Often such activities might, in reality, serve to stem one's creative flow. But neither does creativity spring from rest alone. We also err whenever we identify creativity with constant inactivity. Rather, true creativity involves a harmonious blending of activity and rest. All other descriptions of creativity are frauds masquerading as the real McCoy. We must step aside to clear our minds and imaginations and to allow fresh ideas and perspectives to live and grow. Then we must return to our activities to give flesh and substance to those ethereal notions. Our ideas and notions are but fleeting, ghostly shadows if not made incarnate. Our programs and products, birthed without reflective thought and creative, imaginative perspective, are but automatons best left dead.

Coming Aside to Rest

The famed English author and mathematician, Lewis Carroll, once penned these lines:

> There comes a pause, for human strength
> Will not endure to dance without cessation;

And everyone must reach the point at length
Of absolute prostration.[21]

Similarly, French essayist Michel de Montaigne once questioned: "Have you known how to take rest? You have done more than he who hath taken empires and cities."[22] Both men evidently knew creation's message: humans cannot work well without rest. To work well, we must find time to rest, or we will exhaust all our resources. This truth applies to all created beings, even those called to minister in God's name. If we want to work well, we must carefully steward our bodily resources. Our bodily resources are our capital. Rest constitutes the God-ordained way to invest our capital to produce greater dividends. Thus, Ernest Hemingway wrote: "I still need more healthy rest in order to work at my best. My health is the main capital I have and I want to administer it intelligently."[23] I wish ministers knew what Hemingway did. Health is our main capital. We have to administer it intelligently and steward it wisely. The evidence suggests we do not know this. That's why we foolishly squander this resource bringing upon ourselves all kinds of physical and emotional ailments.

I do not speak of Sabbath rest here as a means of promoting our spiritual well-being. I speak of rest as a cessation of our activity. I do so not to disparage spiritual rest. There's ample evidence for this throughout Scripture. I choose the former emphasis for two reasons: First, it's the emphasis in Genesis. Second, while we may acknowledge the need to rest for spiritual reasons, we may ignore the call to retreat when made solely for physical considerations.

This bifurcation is unfortunate. Rest for worship and resting for health reasons are inseparable twins. In fact, rest can serve both purposes simultaneously. Sometimes we retreat to steward our physical health. In the process we discover our spiritual lives have received unexpected benefits. Sometimes we retreat for spiritual reasons and find this respite, however brief, recharged our entire beings. It's because we are systems. Anything affecting our bodies has implications for our spirits. Likewise, neglecting our spirits has a detrimental impact on our bodies.

Rest has other spiritual connections. As indicated earlier, ceasing our activity signifies confidence in God. We trust Him to continue acting even when our labors have ended. It's a real truth worth putting into practice. Unfortunately, it has become, in many places a forgotten one. We often exhaust ourselves with constant activity because we believe it's all up to us. In reality, it's all up to God.

1. Walter Brueggemann, *Genesis* (Atlanta: John Knox Press, 1982), p. 24.
2. Václav Havel, in an acceptance speech, Germany, October 1989, quoted in *Independent*, London, December 9, 1989, from *The Columbia Dictionary of Quotations* (New York: Columbia University Press, 1993).
3. Raymond J. Corsini and Danny Wedding. *Current Psychotherapies*, 4th Edition (Itasca, IL: F.E. Peacock, 1989), p. 3.
4. William Willimon, "The Power of Mere Words," *Leadership* 21:1 (Winter 2000), pp. 29-30.
5. Murray Bowen, *Family Therapy in Clinical Practice* (New York: J. Aronson, 1978).
6. Robert Morgan, "The Need to Be Needed," *Building Your Church through Counsel and Care: 30 Strategies to Transform Your Ministry*, ed. Marshall Shelley (Minneapolis, MN: Bethany House, 1997), pp. 83-89 at 86.
7. 1991 Survey of Pastors, Fuller Institute of Church Growth, in H.B. London and Neil B. Wiseman, *Pastors at Risk* (Wheaton, IL: Victor Books, 1993).
8. David Goetz, "Is the Pastor's Family Safe at Home?" *Leadership* 13:4 (Fall 1992): pp. 38-44 at 39.
9. Donald E. Gowan, *From Eden to Babel: A Commentary on the Book of Genesis 1-11* (Grand Rapids, MI: Eerdmans, 1988).
10. Brueggemann, *Genesis*. I have modified the order to reflect the ordering in the narrative.
11. J. Philip Newell, *Celtic Benediction* (Grand Rapids, MI: Eerdmans, 2000), p. 76.
12. Richard Foster, *Celebration of Discipline* (San Francisco: Harper, 1998), p. 27.
13. Bruce Reed, *Dynamics of Religion* (London: Darton, Longman and Todd, 1978).
14. Shawchuck, Norman and Roger Heuser, *Leading the Congregation: Caring for Yourself While Serving the People* (Nashville: Abingdon, 1993), pp. 46-47.
15. G.B. Trudeau, *Doonesbury*, dist. by Universal Press Syndicate, *Lexington Herald Leader*, March 10, 1996.
16. Brueggemann, *Genesis*, p. 35
17. Eugene Peterson, *Working the Angles: The Shape of Pastoral Integrity* (Grand Rapids, MI: Eerdmans, 1987).
18. Brueggemann, *Genesis*, p. 35.
19. Ibid.
20. David Benner, *Sacred Companions* (Downers Grove, IL: Intervarsity Press, 2002), pp. 46-47.

21. Lewis Carroll, *Four Riddles*, no. 1 (first published 1869; reproduced in *Phantasmagoria and Other Poems*, 1919), from *The Columbia Dictionary of Quotations* (New York: Columbia University Press, 1993).
22. Michel de Montaigne, "Of Experience," Essays, bk. 3, ch. 13, tr. John Florio (1588), from *The Columbia Dictionary of Quotations* (New York: Columbia University Press, 1993).
23. Ernest Hemingway, Letter, Feb. 21, 1952, published in *Selected Letters*, ed. Carlos Baker (1981), from *The Columbia Dictionary of Quotations* (New York: Columbia University Press, 1993, 1995, 1998, 1999).

Chapter 8

The Disciplines of Ministry

Starting Well, Finishing Strong

Starting well and finishing strong doesn't just happen. It's a matter of discipline. Any athlete would attest to this truth. But discipline doesn't only apply to sports. It applies to all human endeavors. It certainly applies to the practice of ministry. The writer of the gospel of Mark evidently knew this. For this reason, he gives us a glimpse into the ministry of Jesus right from the start. We catch a brief hint of this ministry in the passage below:

> At that time Jesus came from Nazareth in Galilee and was baptized by John in the Jordan. As Jesus was coming up out of the water, he saw heaven being torn open and the Spirit descending on him like a dove. And a voice came from heaven: "You are my Son, whom I love; with you I am well pleased." At once the Spirit sent him out into the desert, and he was in the desert forty days, being tempted by Satan. He was with the wild animals, and angels attended him. (Mark 1:9-14 NIV)

These verses and those which follow provide key insights into the disciplines which shaped Jesus' ministry. By investigating this passage we can gain new perspectives which might reshape ministry. Informed by these we may learn to reframe ministry in ways which promote a kinder, gentler approach. This approach would help ministers combine compassion for others with self-compassion and self-care. We can detect this approach in the disciplines Jesus observed. That's the focus of this chapter.

The Discipline of a Spirit-Empowered Life

Jesus knew that the Holy Spirit empowers ministry. No wonder the presence and power of the Holy Spirit loomed large throughout His ministry. The Holy Spirit's prominence manifests itself right from the beginning of Mark's gospel. This is surprising given the Spirit is rarely mentioned in the rest of the gospel. In fact, Mark directly refers to the Holy Spirit only six times, three of which appear in the prologue. In 1:8, the author mentions the coming of the Spirit-baptism; in 1:10, he portrays Jesus as the model for one baptized with the Spirit; and in 1:12-13, the Spirit leads Jesus into the wilderness.[1] Mark scatters the other three references throughout the remainder of the gospel (3:39, 12:36 and 13:11). Why this prominence in the prologue? Craig Keener contends that this is so because Mark wishes us to assume the Spirit's presence throughout the entire book. He wants us to know that the Spirit's presence and power pervaded every aspect of Jesus' life and activities, including His confrontation with evil.[2]

We see this pervasive presence in several places. With the image of the dove-like Spirit found in Mark 1:10, the Spirit implicitly proclaims Jesus as the founder of a new order, and as the Messiah who ushers in the Spirit and the kingdom.[3] Two images of the Spirit mark this passage. First, we encounter the Spirit as a gentle, affirming presence who engenders power in Christ's life throughout His ministry. In this power, Jesus would bring healing to those most in need of it. With it, He would combat demons and drive them out from those caught in their clutches.

Second, the passage portrays the Spirit leading Jesus into trial and suffering. In Mark 1:12, the Spirit drives Jesus into the wilderness. Significantly, the word used in both places is the same one used for driving out demons. The word conjures up images of the great might and force evident in the Spirit. This contrasts with the gentle image mentioned earlier. But Christ responded to both forms of the Spirit's leadership: He responded to the gentle presence and the power He received. He willingly followed the Spirit's forceful leadership into paths of suffering.

The Spirit's Power in Our Ministry

The Spirit's role in Christ's ministry teaches at least three fundamental truths. First, it reminds us that effectiveness in ministry is ultimately not up to us; rather, effectiveness springs from an indwelling Spirit who inhabits the lives of faithful servants. This truth alone should help us reframe ministry from one which is person-empowered and dependent on the minister's skills, ability, efforts and charisma, to one which is ultimately Spirit-empowered. Second, it teaches the importance of the Holy Spirit's presence and power in our ministry. Without the Spirit's presence we are ill-equipped for ministry and can expect to fail eventually. Third, Christ's baptism with the Spirit makes real our own baptism. The hope of the Spirit's power and presence is not a pipe dream. Because of His own baptism, Jesus is uniquely qualified to give the Spirit to His followers. This is the reality to which John the Baptist pointed when he spoke of Jesus as the One who would baptize with the Holy Spirit. He stands ready to impart the Spirit to those who engage the demonic powers of this world in His name. No wonder He commanded His disciples to wait until they were endued with power from on high.

Unfortunately, too many ministers desire the Spirit's power but shun His transforming presence. A minister once told me a story which provides a disturbing example of this contradiction. "Marty" had been reared in a church which emphasized power and varied manifestations of the Spirit. Sadly, according to him, the church leaders misused power: they lied, they intimidated and exploited members for their own gain; they cut them off from dissenting voices. He himself had been deeply wounded by the church's leadership. As a result, he bristled with intense anger anytime he heard preachers talk like these leaders did. Besides their abuses, these leaders demonstrated great disparity between their public persona and their private lives. In public, they emphasized the Spirit's power; in private, they betrayed the Spirit's transforming presence by their conduct: participating in liaisons with women other than their wives, indulging in questionable sexual jokes at private parties, and lacing their conversations with racist talk. One wonders which "spirit" inhabited their lives. Their habits bear little resemblance to a life lived in obedience to the Holy Spirit.

If we desire the Spirit's power, we must discipline ourselves to seek His presence and radically obey His directives. Such obedience carries implications for our public and private lives. It demands consistency between our real selves and our professional persona. We can't live like Jekyll and Hyde. We can't appear respectable and saintly in public, but live like devils in private. We must strive to bring our private lives into congruence with our public claims. This congruence provides a powerful witness to others, but it does more: it largely eliminates the personal fragmentation which occurs when we behave radically different in public than we do in private.

The Discipline of Intimacy with God

We can only experience the continual presence and power of the Spirit by cultivating intimacy with God. No wonder intimacy with God characterized Christ's life! He knew humans were created to have close, intimate contact with God. Therefore, he sought constant and close intimacy with the Father. Mark portrays this intimacy in glorious detail at the beginning of his gospel. God Himself witnessed to the intimacy by act and affirmation. First, He bore witness to His intimacy with the Son through the gift of the dove-like Spirit. Then He confirmed it by affirmation: "You are my Son, whom I love; with you I am well pleased" (1:11b NIV). The whole scene is pregnant with intimacy. It is generally believed that Jesus alone saw the heavens open and the Spirit descending. From this perspective, Jesus and His Father shared a moment intended for their eyes and ears alone. The scene reminds me of two lovers sharing a private gesture in public. The gesture, whether seen or unseen by others, is primarily for the couple. The act speaks intimacy and meanings of which the couple alone is truly aware.

The affirmations reinforce intimacy. The Father affirmed Jesus as the Son. In this context, "Son" signified His unique relationship with the Father.[4] God owned His Son in whom He found unbounded pleasure. Being a father of three sons, I understand this well. Like any parent, there are times of exasperation. But these times are few compared with the sheer joy I experience in watching them grow. God's affirmation is like this: He rejoices in His Son and the pleasure He brings. The pleasure partly springs from the Son's obedience. But there is more. God sees in Him all He intends for His Son to be. He looks at Jesus and asks for nothing more. In this affirmation, "You are my Son, whom I love; with you I am well pleased," we find deep love and unqualified approval just because He is the Son. The approval had little to do with His performance in ministry, for such service had not yet begun. This love and approval defined and grounded Jesus' identity. He knew Himself as the Father's Beloved. With this knowledge and assurance, He could face any trial or temptation without faltering. He did not need to prove His identity to Satan. He already knew Himself to be the Son of God. With an identity firmly grounded in God, He could pursue ministry with unmixed motives. He did not need to use ministry as an opportunity to define His own identity or bolster His self-esteem.

Intimacy Depends on Intentional Spirituality

Jesus' intimacy with the Father didn't happen haphazardly. It developed from intentional design and flourished by disciplined habit. That's always true. True intimacy with God never happens without intention and discipline. It comes by intentional spirituality. According to Hands and Fehr, spirituality refers to the "...concrete way of living in conscious relationship to the mystery of God."[5] It involves the awareness of God at work in human life. It likewise includes the various means of grace by which we keep awareness alive. Its ultimate goal is to transform us into the very image of Christ.[6] But spirituality isn't just a solitary activity. It's also formed within community.[7] We cultivate spirituality through processes which are both private and communal. These include habits like prayer, Bible reading and worship. Sometimes, these practices take place in our "secret places," when we get alone with God. Sometimes they occur in the community of faith. For example, family worship, accountability groups and the worshipping community are all means through which Christ is formed in us. These behaviors and habits serve to develop and enhance the awareness of God in our lives. We ought not to avoid such habits, believing they are too mechanical and routine. But neither should we see these as the ultimate goals. The ultimate purpose is inner transformation of our being. Without such transformation, we are like Pharisees engaged in empty rituals possessing no life-changing power .

The Spirituality of Jesus

Jesus cultivated these habits intentionally. We see intention in Christ's presentation for water baptism in Mark 1:9. Because He lived a completely holy life, there was nothing personal from which to repent. His repentance derived from standing in our place.[8] This act revealed both His intentions on our behalf and the humility of His spiritual walk. We see this in the contrasts between the two baptisms in verses 8 and 9. Jesus brought the Spirit's baptism, greater than the water baptism John offered. Why then did the One with the greater gift submit to one with the lesser gift? Because of His humility! Christ knew His greater destiny, but did not allow it to cloud His present behavior.

We can learn a great deal from Christ's example. We learn that future visions of greatness need not foster present haughtiness. I have known of ministers who possessed a sense of destiny. From the time God called them, they knew His grand designs for them. Standing in their presence, one could sense potential greatness. But future visions clouded the present and made them despise the day of small things. Sometimes visions of the big things blinded them to the little stuff to which God now called them. They did not seem to realize that small things were preparations for the big things. Sometimes they saw the little things, but either ignored them or complained about the humble tasks dotting their paths. Sometimes, chomping at the bit to get to the glory, they avoided obligations which appeared inconsequential when compared to their visions. Not Christ! He knew He had a greater baptism, yet this did not stop Him from submitting to John's baptism.

Other acts of intentional spirituality appear in Mark 1. His time away in the wilderness speaks of intentional behavior. Clearly this event was important for His spiritual well-being and His mission. According to Lane, "…sonship must be reaffirmed in the wilderness."[9] Some authors refer to this as the testing of the hero. Another intentional act is the time Jesus spent praying, found in 1:35. This reference is significant because Mark only mentions three occasions where Jesus is actually seen praying (also 6:46; 14:32-42). Nevertheless, we get the sense that this was a cultivated and constant habit. This and other habits were the means by which He maintained contact with the Father.

In *Leading the Congregation: Caring for Yourself while Serving the People*, Shawchuck and Heuser suggest three elements in the spirituality of Jesus. First, His spirituality was cultivated through a small group of disciples. Second, Jesus used the means of grace to shape His spirituality: He "...taught by example that six graces were vital to his life and ministry: prayer, fasting, the Lord's Supper, the Scriptures, spiritual conversation and worship in the Temple. These he incorporated into the fabric of his life in order to sustain his ministry."[10] Third, as part of His spirituality, Jesus established "a rhythm of public ministry and private time."[11]

The spirituality of Jesus implies several things for us. It calls us away from finding spirituality only in the crowd. We often do this when we base our spiritual lives on our professional life and functions. Furthermore, Jesus' example reminds us of our need for intimate relationships with select others. Real intimacy rarely occurs in large gatherings where we can easily hide behind our professional masks. Rather, the intimacy which enhances spirituality normally occurs in small covenant groups. No wonder Jesus carved out a smaller group, consisting of Peter, James and John, within the Twelve. Jesus obviously knew the truth about small intimate groups. Ministers, especially the wildly extroverted, tend to substitute the constant frenzy of the crowd for small covenant relationships. Rarely do they find place for "the rhythm of public ministry and private time." Public ministry calls forth images of the crowds; private time speaks of solitude. This rhythm is absolutely necessary for healthy ministry. Too many ministers only play the music of the crowd. They know little of the music composed in solitude.

Intimacy with God in Ministry

From this discussion of intimacy, we may readily see its implications for life and ministry. Intimacy with God brings us to the realization of our truest identity. We never truly know ourselves until we see ourselves through the eyes of God. Since God is the One who made us, we can only discover the full meaning of our identity in Him. The discovery most critical to identity is to know ourselves as God's beloved. But this never happens until we come into true intimacy with God. At the same time, intimacy with God permits self-intimacy. For Hands and Fehr, "...intimacy with God is really the indispensable accompaniment of true intimacy with self."[12] They note that intimacy with God requires self-respect, self-compassion, self-nurture and self-love. These qualities create a stance making intimacy with God possible.

The discovery of identity carries implications for motivations in ministry. Until we discover ourselves in God, we often try to forge our identity by performance. Henri Nouwen suggests that unless we know ourselves as the beloved, we can easily become addicted to success and accomplishments. We can become slaves to the accolades of crowds rather than the free servants of God.[13] In a similar vein, the authors of *Spiritual Wholeness for Clergy* note that the discovery of being loved by God should take priority over all other ways of relating to God. Until we discover His unconditional love, life and ministry easily become distorted and driven. In contrast, knowing His love, and thereby discovering ourselves, we can serve as persons who labor out of love for God and His creatures. In this sense, intimacy with God purifies our motives. Without it, ministry can degenerate into an egoistic need to define and prove ourselves to others. In turn, this colors everything we do, even the things we do in ministry.[14]

Pursuing Intimacy with God

Ministers ought to pursue intimacy with God for personal reasons, not professional ones. Personal spirituality is all about relating to God *for our own sake*. It focuses attention on our own need for God, on a personal desire to know His love and experience His transforming presence. This desire stimulates us to cultivate the spiritual disciplines as means of transforming us into God's image. But we can seek intimacy for professional reasons. We do so whenever we primarily seek contact with God *for the sake of others*.[15] Sporadic encounters with God occur as a result of serving others. Disciplines like prayer and Scripture reading become public events meant to uplift and inspire others. Our personal need for God fades into the background. We mistakenly hope the public display of spirituality will contribute to more intimate contact with God. But intimacy with God doesn't happen this way. Intimacy with God demands a personal touch and relating to God for ourselves. This doesn't mean nothing spiritual happens when we minister to others. But one cannot develop true intimacy with God if one is always relating to God *through* others. Neither can we spiritually sustain ourselves with crumbs from another's table.

Lack of Intimacy and Problems in Ministry
When we fail to develop intimacy with God, we invariably encounter problems. These problems are glaringly apparent in *Spiritual Wholeness for Clergy*. The authors' insights flow directly from their work with real-life clergy. For several years they directed the Barnabas Center, a program for clergy. The ministers who came to the center had "hit bottom." They had experienced burnout, been engaged in extra-marital affairs or addictions which posed a hazard to their lives and ministries. Despite these differences, they shared a common trait: they lacked personal intimacy with God. They had become alienated from God and themselves. Yet, they still attempted to speak eloquently about a mystery which had long been lost to them.[16]

Inevitably, loss of intimacy created problems. They brought these difficulties to the Barnabas Center. The problems stemmed from vain attempts to fill the void in their lives with poor substitutes. Wine, women and workaholic behavior were all attempts to fill the void which God alone could fill. Given their detachment from God, some became spiritual impostors. The authors called them "Sons of Sceva." Though they outwardly appeared as servants of God, they were impostors. They sought power from God apart from close contact with Him. Others displayed a kind of reverse pride meant to substitute for their lack of truly knowing God. Still others developed religious addictions masquerading as intimacy. Like leeches, they clung to God to make up for their lack of power. The innocent onlooker could easily mistake this behavior for true intimacy, but it wasn't. It lacked deep and personal contact with God. In reality, it was nothing more than compulsive involvement in religious things and spiritual activities.[17]

Sometimes, this lack of intimacy contributes to a "split between head and heart." The split shows itself most when our public, godly persona covers a private life that is anything but godly. It evidences itself in compulsive habits and over-responsible behavior, and in narcissistic quests for attention and the messiah-like need to be all things to all people.[18] Strangely enough, these patterns don't deliver. Rather, they contribute to spiritual self-deception whereby we sanctify our workaholic tendencies with spiritual labels.

Self-deception is but one price we pay for failing to cultivate intimacy with God. Hands and Fehr highlight other problems, such as pouring out spiritual nourishment to others without replenishing ourselves, or speaking eloquently about the spiritual life without living it. We sometimes become addicted to work and tangible substances in order to shield ourselves from our pain. Ultimately, we can pay the greatest price of all—the loss of faith.[19] Each of these examples represents self-avoidance or self-neglect. This should not surprise us. Unless we know God intimately, we cannot come to self-intimacy. Unless we know God, we cannot discover our identity as His beloved. Earlier I showed how the discovery of ourselves as God's beloved affects motivations in ministry. But that's not its only importance. Until we know ourselves as God's beloved, we tend to treat ourselves as worthless things. We think that everyone else is beloved and worthy of care, but not us. Until we discover ourselves as God's beloved, we will continue to exhibit behaviors which loudly proclaim our lack of worth and need for care and love.

Unfortunately, we sometimes come to intimacy with God and ourselves through a hard, remedial way. Those who came to the Barnabas Center had to "hit bottom"; they had to be brought low. They had to fail in some noticeable way so they could discover they did not have it all together. I call it "hitting bottom" because the description of these clergy parallels that of alcoholics. Usually, alcoholics must totally crash in order to discover their ruinous condition. It's this recognition which paves the road to recovery. Likewise, bankrupt ministers need to discover their spiritual poverty if they want to carve out a new relationship with God. From the depths of this ruin, they have an opportunity to discover God's unconditional love for them. This remedial path to intimacy is not God's design. He prefers we come to closeness *before* we fall. But it's good to know there is a path to restoration of our spiritual lives and our human identity. It's the same one He charted from the time of creation—total, radical intimacy with God.

The Discipline of Solitude and Retreat

In contrast, Jesus knew ministry demanded solitude and retreat. Besides its obvious benefits to spiritual and overall well-being, two troublesome ministry characteristics make solitude necessary. Ministry has the tendency to consume all our energies. At the same time, it can rob us of personal identity. The constant demands tempt us to find our identity in what we do rather than who we are. For these reasons, solitude and retreat make a great deal of sense. Solitude serves to replenish our limited resources so we can return refreshed to the tasks that beckon us. At the same time, solitude reminds us of our identity as children of God who need time alone with Him.

I use the word "solitude" in a broad sense. I include those times when the minister is truly on his own. These include times of silence, reading of God's word, meditation and personal prayer. I also include those occasions when the minister retreats with small groups (such as in accountability situations). Jesus evidently used both. In Mark 1:12, under the Spirit's guidance, Jesus retreated to be alone. We find a similar reference in Mark 1:35: "Very early in the morning, while it was still dark, Jesus got up, left the house and went off to a solitary place, where he prayed" (NIV). Other references to personal, private retreat appear in 1:45 and 6:45. Commentators suggest that in Mark 6:1, Jesus went to Nazareth for rest, not preaching. From this perspective, the preaching done represents an accommodation to the crowd, not Jesus' true intention.[20] Jesus also retreated with His disciples. Jesus used these times to foster contact with God and to form community among His disciples. These times of solitude set the foundation for Jesus' public ministry.

This emphasis on rest and retreat in Mark may surprise many. Many of us have been taught that Mark's gospel emphasizes action. That is true! Mark has appropriately been called the "Gospel of Action." The Greek word translated "straightway," or "immediately," appears 40 to 50 times, depending on textual variations.[21] However, amidst the drama and fast-paced action, we should not miss the subtle emphasis on rest and solitude. Like no other gospel writer, Mark highlights Jesus seeking solitude. Vincent notes that this gospel records at least eleven occasions where Jesus sought solitude.[22] The reasons are varied. Sometimes He retired from His work to escape His enemies. Other times He sought privacy to pray, or to rest. Still other times, He sought private conference with His disciples. But we often do not pay enough attention to this emphasis on rest and retreat. Much of the time, it gets lost in the hubbub of Mark's activity. But it is there nonetheless. By seeking balance between action and rest, community and solitude, Jesus followed a fundamental principle observed in creation: activity must continually be interspersed with rest as a basis for personal renewal and true creativity.

Significantly, solitude and retreat play a role in the structure of Mark's gospel. Each phase of Jesus' ministry to others begins with retreat. For example, the first phase in Galilee begins in 1:14, and runs through 3:6. This phase is preceded by a time of withdrawal (Mark 1:9-13). The later phase of the Galilean ministry begins in 3:7, and extends through 6:13.[23] This section also begins with withdrawal (Mark 3:7). Evidently, Mark means to communicate an important dynamic of ministry from this parallel structure. For Mark, solitude and intimate contact with God should precede ministry to others. This seems a fundamental part of his theology of ministry. Solitude and retreat represent the first movement in ministry. It is first because it provides a foundation for service to others. Once we have cared for our own well-being, spiritually and otherwise, we are in good shape to begin the second movement—the ministry we provide to others.

Jesus found wonderful places for retreat. He used solitary wilderness places, the mountains and the sea. From experience, all of these are wonderful places to promote undisturbed contact with the divine. Several years ago, I lived on the island of Dominica. Dominica is a rugged country of mountains, rivers and cool mountain streams. Dominicans boast that they have 365 rivers, one for every day of the year. I lived way out in the country, about three miles from the nearest village. About a mile down the road from the campus where I lived was a river we simply called "the Big River." The river lay off to one side of the road. To get to it, one had to take a small winding trail down to the river. And what a wonderful place! Cool, crystal clear water—so clear, one felt one could almost reach out and touch the very bottom. The river was encircled in lush, green vegetation, and sparkling vistas—a modern-day garden of Eden. A true place of retreat! The river ran shallow in places, with large stones jutting out of the water. I could easily walk out into the middle of the river by stepping on these stones. This was my private place of retreat. For about two years, I spent half my Saturday mornings fasting, praying and reading the Word. This was my place of retreat with God. I would step out onto the stones, find a place in the middle of the river to sit, and there commune with God. What times of refreshing! I must confess that, at times, I have wished that I had a "Big River" nearby. The closest I have come to this experience was on a boat trip with my friend Mark to Cave Run Lake. Cave Run Lake is a man-made lake nestled among the mountains of Eastern Kentucky. On this evening, we pulled out from the marina and headed out into the lake. As the sun began to set, we pulled off onto a rocky, island-like shore. There, in the deepening evening light, we lit a fire and roasted salmon. As we sat talking, one could look into the sky and count the brightly glistening stars. I have never been able to find the Big Dipper easily. Out there on Cave Run Lake, it gleamed big and clear—impossible to miss. In those moments, I envisioned Jesus being in such a place. I could sense that in such a place, one could easily feel the presence of God. At least I could. No wonder Jesus chose the mountains and the sea.

Solitude Is Not Wasted Time

Sometime ago, I ran across a seminarian's spouse in a local store. Our spring reading week had just come to an end. I asked her how her family had spent the time. Rather nonchalantly, she told me they had done nothing. As it turned out, this "nothing" was a family trip to the Smoky Mountains. They had rented a cottage high up in the mountains. By design, they brought no television, no radio or other media tool to disturb their private retreat. They spent their time playing games, having fun, renewing and reinvigorating their contact with each other. This was far from "nothing." They were involved in some of the most important work they could do.

Sometimes ministers make a similar mistake. They call times of solitude wasted time. They are wrong. Solitude is something.

It's designed to replenish our whole being. Time aside is not merely the edges. It is really the center and heart of ministry. It is problematic that so many find it peripheral, when it is so central to personal wholeness and effective ministry. But because many ministers count it wasted time, they often do not exert the effort to retreat from the busyness of their lives.

Many reasons give rise to this problem. First, by word and deed, many of us mistakenly associate ministry with constant busyness. Not too long ago I spoke to an associate minister of a very large church. The church had gone through a recent change in pastoral leadership. During our conversation we spoke about the stresses of ministry and the difficulty of balancing all the pieces. This minister affirmed his appreciation for the new senior minister. His appreciation stemmed from the senior pastor's support and encouragement of personal and family time. In contrast, the former minister modeled constant busyness and expected the same of his associates.

Second, we often mimic the culture in which we live. Our culture encourages and lauds constant busyness. It marches to the drum of continual activity and madding crowds. Our culture disdains and even avoids solitude. Besides societal influence, many ministers simply do not know how to be alone. A close friend and colleague illustrated this with a story of a depressed minister who came to an eminent psychiatrist for help. The psychiatrist required the minister to go home and spend time with himself. During the week, the minister spent time reading his favorite authors and listening to his favorite musicians. At the end of the week he returned, still depressed. Asked whether he had faithfully completed the assignment, he told about his reading and music time. "That's not what I told you," replied the psychiatrist. "I told you to spend time with yourself." The minister retorted, "You mean just be alone with me. I couldn't do that." The psychiatrist drove his dagger home: "And yet you will foist yourself on innocent parishioners all week long." I do not know the truth of the story. It could well be apocryphal. Yet it illustrates a sad truth: many ministers do not know how to be alone or how to enjoy solitude. So we stay constantly busy, driven by a latent desire to escape ourselves.

Solitude may even become a reason for drivenness and busyness. Fred, a successful minister, once shared with me a story about a very hectic time in his ministry. He had thoroughly exhausted himself. He decided he desperately needed a break and finally decided to head to a nearby monastery. Having grown accustomed to busyness, he undermined his purpose by taking two briefcases of work. At the monastery, a monk met him and inquired about the briefcases. "I wanted to get away so I could get some paperwork done," he replied. The monk prevailed upon him to leave the cases in his car. Fred went to his room intending to rise within the hour to eat dinner and get to his work. He never made it to that meal. He slept through the whole time. His body and mind were exhausted. He had not heard his body talk amidst the din of constant busyness.

Finally, some of us value and require solitude, but feel guilty about taking such time. It's almost as if we see our need for solitude as a bad thing. I have seen this phenomenon all too often. I have met ministers whose very demeanor loudly proclaimed their need for solitude. But they disparaged and disowned the need. Instead, they found additional occasions demanding involvement with others. I remember a similar time in graduate school when an insightful professor highlighted a similar tension in my life. He said to me, "Most people think you are an extrovert, but I suspect that you are much more introverted than it appears." By these comments, he implied the introvert's need for privacy and solitude. Initially, I was almost offended by his comments. I had fallen prey to the cultural values which exalt the extrovert's frenzied activity, while despising the introvert's need for solitude and retreat. But later, as I reflected on his comments, I knew he was right. I could look back over my life and see the strong preference for times of solitude. I could easily be with people, but also needed privacy for my own well-being. Thankfully, I have learned how to value this side of my personality and make solitude work for me. Amidst work which demands a great deal of time with people, it has been my salvation.

The Discipline of Faithfulness

Jesus demonstrated that ministry depends on the disciplines of obedience and faithfulness. Mark 1:12-13 highlights Jesus' testing in the wilderness. Such periods of testing seem to characterize many devout servants of God. Some call these "wilderness experiences." In the Old Testament, Moses experienced a 40-day stay on Mt. Sinai and 40 years herding sheep. Elijah experienced 40 days of wandering through the wilderness of Mt. Horeb. Such times seem to benefit ministry by testing our submission to the Father's will. They prove our mettle in the midst of temptation. Will the servant of God remain faithful through suffering? Will the minister hold fast to God in spite of the darkness? Will the man or woman of God resist every attack of Satan? These are the kinds of questions which are often answered only by the wilderness experience. Before beginning His ministry, Jesus had to stand the test of faithfulness and integrity, so the Spirit drove Jesus to this place of testing.

As I indicated earlier, in this passage, there is a strange contrast in the Spirit's actions. The Spirit is seen both as a gentle, dove-like presence and a sort of taskmaster driving the Beloved to the wilderness. We might wish to destroy one of these images because they appear contradictory. Yet both are valid. They represent the tough and tender actions of the Spirit—both consistent with a Father's love. The servant of God must learn to respond to both. We must learn to own, feel and acknowledge the gentle affirmations. But we must also learn to accept the directions which seem not to make sense. We must obediently follow the Spirit into paths that appear harsh and unnecessary, and which we would not choose for ourselves. Jesus responded to both directions. He had first accepted the Spirit's gentle presence. Now He accepted the Spirit's path to the wilderness. This submission to the Father's will meant days of deprivation, temptation and confrontation by Satan, exposure to wild beasts and the harsh elements of nature. Jesus endured it all. He stood the test and proved Himself faithful. How easy it would have been to resist this harsh leading of the Spirit! Had He not already been approved as the Beloved Son? Had God not confirmed His pleasure with Jesus? These images fit better with a benign and glorious path. Why now this austere setting? These are the kinds of questions many ministers ask when confronting difficulties. Many of us seek to shun this rugged path. Not Jesus! He knew that being the Beloved Son did not exempt Him from times of suffering and humiliation. Those of us who want to follow God fully cannot abandon the wilderness experiences. We must remain until God directs us to leave.

This kind of faithfulness and obedience doesn't just happen. Faithfulness under fire proceeds from cultivated intimacy with God forged through intentional spiritual formation. Some servants of God buckle under stress, temptations and the demands of ministry. They do not maintain faithfulness and integrity under fire. In many cases, the fault lies squarely at their door. They have not sought to cultivate an intimacy with God that produces maximum staying power. Neither do they practice intentional spiritual formation. Their spirituality is largely professional, rather than personal. Professional spirituality will not endure the fires of temptation and testing for long.

A Table in the Wilderness

God honors obedience and faithfulness. Significantly, besides the temptation and austerity of the wilderness, Mark also recorded its blessing, making a passing reference to the angel's ministry to Jesus (Mark 1:13). As He did with Elijah (1 Kings 19:5-7), God sustained Jesus in the wilderness by the presence and ministry of angels. This service by angels serves to highlight the humanity of Jesus. The context does not say in what ways they ministered to Him. However, it is fair to assume that their ministry included serving His physical needs. Given Jesus' extensive time in this place, and the spiritual, mental and emotional duress, these needs must have been considerable. But God sent the angels. In both Elijah's and Jesus' experience, God reminds us of a comforting fact: He never forgets the human needs of His servants. The image of the ministering angels affirms another point: God will prove Himself faithful with those who live faithfully. He does not desert His own. He does not desert us in our times of need.

I suspect if we observed these same disciplines, our practice of ministry would be different. For one, we would learn to reframe ministry as an activity wholly dependent upon intimate contact with God through the Spirit. Having done that, we would show more diligence and intention in shepherding our own spirituality and well-being. We would learn to carve out time for retreat and solitude rather than staying constantly busy. In the process, we would discover a power and stamina which helps us complete the tasks to which God calls us. Such disciplines would likely alleviate, if not eliminate, the burnout which brings many a ministry to a premature end.

The Discipline of Pastoral Care to One's Family

Before concluding, I will highlight another significant issue evident in this first chapter of Mark. This principle involves the role of family in the practice of ministry. Ministry begins with attending to one's own needs. But ministry does not stop there. It should proceed outward in ever-widening circles—even to the ends of the earth. Unfortunately, in their zeal to get to the ends of the earth, ministers too often miss a vital stop. They miss ministering to their nearest neighbors—their families. Mark's gospel provides some insights into this area. One gets the impression that, for Mark, family is not forgotten in the press of serving others.

Two incidents involving family occur in Mark 1, both having to do with men whom Jesus had called to ministry. The first involves the call of James and John. The brothers immediately responded to Jesus call, yet made sure to leave their father in the hands of the hired servants. Some view this as merely a pictorial trait, but others see in it a touch of humanity.[24] James and John responded to Christ's call, but they also made provision for their father's care. The second incident occurs in Mark 1:29. Jesus, together with Peter, Simon, James and John, retired to Peter's house. This suggests that, in the midst of ministry, Christ did not keep His disciples from contact with their families. Indeed, some believe Peter's house served as their headquarters. It was to this place that they frequently retreated. Thus, the door referred to in 1:33 is thought to be the door of Peter's house.[25] Furthermore, an incident at Peter's house provided an opportunity for ministry. Peter's mother-in-law lay sick in bed with a high fever. Alerted to her condition, Jesus healed her. Amidst the rapid-fire healings in Mark 1, time and place was found for a minister's family needs. How significant!

Neglect constitutes one of the greatest complaints from ministers' spouses and families. Ministers often find little time and opportunity to serve their families' needs. Bent on serving others, they often forget those at their own door. This neglect, whether benign or deliberate, has devastating consequences. It most often leads to bitterness and resentment on the part of clergy spouses and children.

Once, during a ministry convention, I overheard a pastor's spouse conversing with her daughter. The spouse related the difficulties of a pastor's life and its negative impact on family. She recounted her husband's busyness, always being on the run and having little time for her and the children. The difficulties were further complicated by the bi-vocational nature of his ministry. She recalled advice she had received from some of the women closest to her. They had warned her of the difficulties of being a pastor's spouse, and had discouraged her from marrying a pastor. The pattern had come full circle. She now gave her daughter the very same advice.

We could easily judge this pastor's wife harshly because she seemingly spoke ill of her husband. Yet she continued to support her husband. During the week, I had seen her fervent service. She obviously loved the Lord and His work, but was deeply hurt by an unavailable husband. She spoke, not so much out of distaste for her husband and ministry, but from reality. For a number of years, she had endured the busyness of a pastor with time for his congregation but little time for her.

Unfortunately, this is sometimes both taught and modeled as a legitimate way to do ministry. Some misguided folk go further and directly endorse neglect of one's family. I referred earlier to an article by John Ortberg, teaching pastor at Willow Creek Community Church, that bears repeating. He recounted a story involving a church-planting consultant. The consultant warned a group of pastors that they would have to pay the price for a successful church plant. "Do what ever it takes: let your marriage suffer, put your children on hold." That was the gist of what he said.[26] Not every church-planting consultant is so foolish and shortsighted. But it is disturbing when even one says such a thing. They obviously do not know Jesus very well. In His deepest agony on the cross, He did not forget His mother. Because He deeply loved her, He entrusted her to John's care. We who minister in His name can do no differently. In the midst of serving others, we mustn't forget the discipline of attending to our families' needs.

1. Craig S. Keener, *The Spirit in the Gospels and Acts* (Peabody, MA: Hendrickson Publishers). See chapter 2, "Jesus as The Spirit Bringer," pp. 49-90.
2. Ibid., p. 50
3. Ibid., pp. 53, 61.
4. Ibid., p. 57. See also W. L. Lane, *The Gospel According to Mark, The New International Critical Commentary on the New Testament* (Grand Rapids, MI: Eerdmans, 1974), p. 57.
5. Hands and Fehr, *Spiritual Wholeness for Clergy: A New Psychology of Intimacy with God, Self and Others* (Washington, D. C.: The Alban Institute, 1993), p. 61.
6. Norman Shawchuck and Roger Heuser, *Leading the Congregation: Caring for Yourself while Serving the People* (Nashville: Abingdon, 1993), p. 119.
7. B.C. Johnson, *Pastoral Spirituality* (Philadelphia: Westminster Press, 1988). p. 23.
8. W. L. Lane, *The Gospel According to Mark, The New International Critical Commentary on the New Testament* (Grand Rapids: Eerdmans, 1974).
9. Ibid., p. 54
10. Shawchuck and Heuser, *Leading the Congregation*, p. 47
11. Ibid., pp. 46-47.
12. Hands and Fehr, *Spiritual Wholeness for Clergy*, p. 70.
13. Henri Nouwen, "From Solitude to Community to Ministry," *Leadership* 16:2 (Spring 1995): pp. 81-87.
14. Hands and Fehr, *Spiritual Wholeness for Clergy*, p. 55.
15. Ibid., pp. 58-65.
16. Ibid., p. 59.
17. Ibid., pp. 51-54.
18. Ibid., p. 55
19. Ibid., pp. 59-60
20. A.B. Bruce, *The Expositor's Greek Testament: The Synoptic Gospels, Volume 1*, ed. W. Robert Nicoll (Grand Rapids, MI: Eerdmans, 1976), pp. 377-378.
21. Lane, *The Gospel According to Mark*, p. 53.
22. Marvin Vincent, *Word Studies in the New Testament, Volumes 1 and 2* (Albany OR: Sage Software, 1996), p. 204. (For example, see Mark 1:12; 3:7; 6:31, 46; 7:24,31; 9:2; 10:1; 14:34).
23. Lane, *The Gospel According to Mark*, p. 29.
24. Bruce, *The Expositor's Greek Testament: The Synoptic Gospels*, p. 344.
25. Ibid., p. 347.
26. John Ortberg, "What's Really Behind Our Fatigue," *Leadership* 18:2 (Spring 1997): 108-113 at 108.

Chapter 9

Principles for the Practice of Ministry

"The real sin against life is to abuse and destroy beauty, even one's own—even more, one's own, for that has been put in our care and we are responsible for its well-being." So wrote novelist Katherine Anne Porter.[1] Porter's words could easily apply to clergy. In the name of serving God, we often destroy our beauty and well-being. While guarding the well-being of others, we show little responsibility for our own welfare. How do we avoid such destructive tendencies? How do we serve effectively without abusing and destroying ourselves? What strategies best preserve and enhance well-being? What strategies guard against personal and family disasters which cripple ministry? The sixth chapter of Mark provides insights which could help us address these types of questions. In fact, Mark provides a wellspring of fundamental principles for practicing ministry. These principles help us stay sane amidst the many demands of ministry. But Mark's principles are not his own. They flow directly from Jesus. We glean them from the directions Jesus gave His disciples both before and after their first unsupervised tour of ministry. Jesus had prepared them well. He had diligently taught them the true meaning of the kingdom and of service. He had given them several opportunities to observe Him. They had seen Him preaching, teaching, healing the sick and casting out devils. Now, Jesus commissioned them to do the same (Mark 6:7-13). And, significantly, their ministry began just as Jesus' did. Earlier, in Mark 6:1, we read that Jesus retreated to His hometown with His disciples, apparently for rest and respite. Like their Master, they would also begin their ministry with retreat.

Principles Based on Reality

To fully comprehend these principles, we need to understand two themes evident in Mark's gospel. These provide a context for appreciating their significance. The first theme involves the realism which pervades Mark's writing. Mark is a "no-nonsense" guy. He tells things as he sees them. He reminds me of Sergeant Friday from the old detective series, *Dragnet*. Sergeant Friday often cautioned his verbose informants to provide "just the facts." Mark writes like a Sergeant Friday. He focuses on facts. However, he paints them with picturesque brilliance. Mark adds details about places, times and people missing in the other gospels. For example, Mark alone records the presence of wild beasts in Jesus' wilderness experience (Mark 1: 13). He alone mentions the use of the fisherman's pillow in Mark 4:38. Moreover, he presents people in authentic detail. From him we learn that James and John were nicknamed "Boanerges," or "Sons of Thunder" (3:17). He alone names the blind man who received his sight. (10:46)[2] Thus, Alexander Bruce writes of Mark: "He describes from the life, avoiding toning down, reticence, generalised [sic] expression, or euphemistic circumlocution."[3]

Realism demands candid depiction of humans with all their frailties and limitations. This realistic depiction even applies to Jesus. In Mark's gospel, "...we get nearest to the human personality of Jesus in all its originality and power and as coloured [*sic*] by the time and the place and the character loses nothing by the realistic presentation."[4] Mark provides everyday encounters with real people, struggling with various needs and wrestling with a variety of emotions. In fact, emotional life stands as one of the distinctive marks of this gospel. Vincent says of Mark: "He abounds in strokes which bring out the *feeling* of his characters."[5] Mark captures the varied emotions of people around him, including Jesus. For example, Mark records the stunned reaction of the people (1:27ff; 2:12); He notes the lack of understanding and hardened hearts of the eyewitness to the miracle of the loaves (6:52). He speaks of the disciples' fear and amazement (9:5ff; 10:24, 32).

We also see Jesus, who exhibits a wide range of emotions (1:41, 43; 3:5, 7:34).[6] Jesus' compassion for varied human needs is a frequent emphasis. The raising of Jairus' daughter is but one glimpse into the compassion of Jesus. The onlookers, astonished by her miraculous resurrection, completely ignored her physical needs. But Jesus did not. He immediately commanded them to give her something to eat (5:43).[7] We see similar concern for hungry people in Mark 6:37. Here, He commanded the disciples to give the crowd something to eat. Yet His compassion extended beyond little girls and hungry crowds. He also showed compassion for those who ministered in His name. Mark 6 provides one such example: in 6:31, Jesus commanded them to come aside for rest and relaxation. He knew the weary disciples needed solitude, rest, and nourishment, just as the hungry crowds needed food. He never forgot the disciples' humanity. Neither must we. To do so invites disaster.

Engagement and Disengagement

In this chapter I have chosen to focus on two portions of Mark chapter 6: verses 7-13 and 30-45. Significantly, in both passages Jesus gives calls which complement and balance each other. In the first, Jesus calls the disciples to engage in ministry. In the second, He commands them to disengage from ministry. Jesus commands us to do both. Zealous disciples quickly discern the voice of God when He calls to engagement. However, we often do not listen or heed His voice when He calls to disengagement. The latter call often seems contrary to His purposes. No wonder we pay little heed to the voice of God which bids us retreat and rest! Sometimes we go even further, attributing the call to disengagement to the devil. In reality, the enemy often seeks to keep us constantly busy. He knows busyness paves the way to a loss of faith. When we so confuse God and Satan, we betray our ignorance of Jesus' ways. His way is the way of balance which fosters creativity. Just as we have seen balance in creation, we also see it in His ministry: He balances activity with retreat; He follows engagement with disengagement. Disengagement is a strategic move, not a full retreat. It allows the forces to muster themselves so they might plunge renewed into the fight.

From these two passages of Scripture, then, I will discuss four principles. From the first section, I will discuss both the need for delegation in ministry and the value of social support. From the second passage, I will focus on the need to regularly lay aside one's role so as to provide self-care and examine the principle of limited resources.

Delegating Ministry to Others

Delegation involves entrusting a person or persons with the responsibility for an activity or task. Successful delegation presumes we also entrust the power to command resources necessary to complete the job. Delegation significantly benefits leaders. It frees them to focus on key concerns while, at the same time, lightening their burdens. We have already seen these basic features implied in Exodus 18. Delegating ministry to others would free Moses to focus on weightier matters. He could represent the people before God and teach them the ways of the Lord. At the same time, he would conserve his energies and enhance his well-being. We see a similar pattern in Acts 6, where the apostles delegated the ministry of serving the widows. This freed them for prayer and the ministry of the Word.

Delegation benefits those entrusted with responsibility. It provides occasion for skill building and developing confidence in one's capacities. It transforms spectators into participants. We see this latter point implied in Exodus 18. The leaders chosen would build skills in judgement. Once they had merely observed—now they would be involved. This new arrangement most likely facilitated speedier judgment which benefited Israel. This must have increased morale among the Israelites. No wonder Jethro said, "If you do this and God so commands, you will be able to stand the strain, and all these people will go home satisfied" (Exodus 18:23 NIV). Similarly, in Acts 6, we see that delegation enhances the skills of those who are chosen. Stephen and Philip provide great examples. Appointed to serve tables, they blossomed and extended their ministry.

Mark 6 presents us with similar delegation. Here, Jesus authorized His disciples to go forth in His word and power. He also invested them with the resources they needed, including power over evil spirits. Because of His trust and confidence in them, twelve more men ministered. This certainly must have lightened the burden for Jesus. But it also benefited the disciples. They became active participants rather than remaining on the sidelines as observers and trainees. Duly authorized, they went out and preached repentance. They exercised their authority in their words and their works: they cast out devils; they healed the sick. In fact, the same evidences which attended Jesus' work now showed in their ministry. One difference existed: whereas Jesus labored in His own power, they operated by borrowed strength—the power of Christ in them.[8] And what a difference it made! They returned rejoicing and amazed at their success.

Delegating Like Jesus

Unfortunately, many pastors do not know how to delegate and, therefore, never try. Sometimes, we do not see delegation as part of our responsibility. Sometimes we do not know how. One pastor readily admitted this. According to him, his style involved "harassing people to do things so we would grow."[9] Delegation is not harassment and browbeating, even when done for a worthy cause. But even when we show a warmer, more congenial approach, we may still err. We often do not trust people enough to provide them the authority and resources to do the job. Lacking these essential tools, it's no wonder they fail. The fault is not theirs, but ours.

Sometimes we understand these principles but experience difficulties because of poor timing. We may delegate before we have provided sufficient training to do the job right. Jesus didn't do this. He sent the Twelve out, but only after He had devoted a great deal of effort and energy to mentoring and discipling them. He taught them about His nature, His mission and the kingdom of God. He modeled the works of the kingdom as He taught and healed and cast out demons. He modeled for them a style of ministry which balanced self-care with service to others. The disciples could easily remember the times Jesus ministered to others. They could remember the times of retreat, rest and solitude devoted to replenishing His soul. What was Jesus' lesson for these and all future leaders? Delegation must always follow discipleship.

Even after investing time in training, however, leadership's work is not complete. Leaders still have obligations. Delegating doesn't let them off the hook completely. They must stay involved. They cannot abdicate responsibility altogether. Eugene Peterson makes this very point. He suggests that pastoral care can be shared, but never delegated. In my opinion, Peterson does not negate delegation per se, but the kind that abdicates responsibility. Thus, he notes that when Moses delegated, he stayed involved. The emphasis is on staying involved.[10] We see this involved delegation in Christ's ministry. That's why the disciples returned to Jesus to give an account of their activities (Mark 6:30). Christian leaders can do no less. They must remain available to provide any additional training needs which arise during the course of ministry. They should provide support and encouragement. They should willingly hear the stories of success and failure and bolster morale when it flags. What's more, they should continue to pray for God to bless and enhance the work of these persons. Ultimately, they should call delegates to give an account to them, all the while reminding them that their ultimate accountability is to God.

Developing Social Support

Besides the call to engagement in Mark 6:7, one should not miss the ministry arrangement found here. Jesus sent the disciples out two by two. Some see this as a means of establishing truth, for according to the law, truth was established in the mouth of two witnesses.[11] Others believe the arrangement highlights the unity among ministers which is essential to promoting the gospel. But a more humane purpose exists: going out in pairs would provide for mutual encouragement and support.[12] Though I do not dismiss the first two explanations, I see the supportive aspects as primary. Jesus sent them out two by two so they might have social support as they conducted ministry.

Social support proceeds from close relationships with others. It's knowing one is loved, valued and connected to others in mutual obligation.[13] We all need this sense of belonging. Without it, humans often feel alone and disconnected. Given the isolating nature of our work, this is particularly true for ministers.[14] In part, it was this need for belonging that led me to change denominations several years ago. There were other reasons, but feelings of disconnection played a large role. It was not an easy decision. I had been a part of my denomination from my conversion. But for several years leading up to the final decision, I had felt disconnected largely because of geography. I lived in Kentucky where my denomination had no churches nearby. Contact with denominational colleagues was all too infrequent. Aside from this, I was close to turning 40, and found connections to be much more important to me at that stage of my life. So, as difficult as it was, I changed to a kindred denomination that provided easier access to a community of faith and support.

Social support serves several important functions. Though it is not a panacea for all our struggles, it functions as a protective mechanism, and helps protect us from feelings of isolation and loneliness. Ayala Pines and her colleagues describe the following functions of social support:

- Listening
- Technical appreciation
- Technical challenge
- Emotional support
- Emotional challenge
- Sharing social reality[15]

These functions readily apply to ministry. Social support can provide ministers with sympathetic ears available to listen to stories of discouragement, failure and success. Given the multiple pressures and demands of ministry, we sometimes have stories we need to share. Unfortunately, ministers often have many critics, but few people who genuinely listen without giving advice or passing judgment. Many times the only support available is from a supportive spouse who also needs a listening ear.

Technical Appreciation and Challenge

Social support also provides technical appreciation and technical challenge. Technical appreciation involves receiving affirmation for a job well done from an acknowledged expert. Having a preaching professor comment on the finer aspects of a good sermon is an example of technical appreciation. Clergy spouses often serve in this capacity for their clergy mates. They cheer their spouses' homiletical efforts. Sometimes they cheer an effort which was not particularly praiseworthy. That's understandable, for that is what many spouses do. Yet, though it is needed and greatly appreciated, it's not technical appreciation. Technical appreciation comes from experts in the field who give honest and candid appraisals.

Additionally, ministers need continual contact with competent colleagues who push them to stay fresh. Colleagues can stretch and encourage one another to greater heights, or challenge each other to innovative thinking. This is technical challenge. It's especially needed when one has served some years in ministry. After a while, freshness and creative energy can wane. Contact with competent colleagues can provide new, reinvigorating challenge.

I saw this illustrated sometime ago by the pastor of a large, thriving church. "Jack" was in his middle years. After many years of successful ministry, he sensed a need for freshness and new direction in his ministry. As a result, he took a year's sabbatical and enrolled in the Beeson Program at Asbury Theological Seminary. The Beeson Program selects and trains bright and promising leaders. Students move through the training as a cohort, becoming steeped in a variety of academic and experiential learning. In the process, they hone their skills as church leaders. I had an occasion to hear Jack speak of his experience. He related how the program had stretched and sharpened him. He had come feeling stale and sensing a need to be re-energized. Through continual contact with students and faculty, he was leaving refreshed, reinvigorated and excited. Beyond the other attractions, he believed the program provided an opportunity for "iron to sharpen iron." He saw this as critical for older ministers needing to evaluate their ministry and its directions. This is a great example of technical challenge.

Emotional Support and Challenge

Furthermore, ministers need emotional support. They need caring individuals who stand with them in difficult situations. Pastors' spouses often provide this support. They are the comforting voice and sympathetic presence pastors often need. But spouses cannot do it alone. Sometimes, shouldering heavy pastoral burdens contributes to their increased stress. Compounding these difficulties, they often have no emotional outlets readily available to them. So, they suffer silently and alone. No wonder so many exhibit greater signs of stress and burnout than their clergy spouses do. They experience a double whammy: they carry their own and their spouses' emotional loads without relief. Moreover, one person cannot possibly meet a minister's emotional support needs. Emotional support is best gained from four to five persons. Perhaps Jesus knew this when He formed His inner circle. In spite of their obvious faults, they likely provided needed support. I suspect Jesus also brought them together to teach them the folly of trying to do ministry as a one-man show.

The demands and pressures of ministry can sometimes muddle our emotions and bias our thinking. At such times, people who lovingly challenge us can help bring us out of our emotional funk. Jethro's challenge to Moses regarding his self-defeating behaviors seems in this vein. Moses had evidently lost sight of important considerations which could have proven detrimental to his health. Jethro's challenge brought him back to reality. God also provided emotional challenge to Elijah in 1 Kings 19. Elijah's fear and isolation had led him to delusional thinking. He believed his persecutors were more powerful than they really were. He believed there were no others like him. God challenged him by pointing him to the truth: his powerful persecutors would meet a quick demise. What's more, he was not alone; there were 7,000 people who had not bowed the knee to Baal. Ministers today often need a similar jolt back to reality.

Sharing Social Reality

Though perceptions can become skewed, sometimes they are real. But given emotional and mental confusion, we can come to doubt the truth of our perceptions. At these times, we need someone to share and help us interpret social reality. Ideally, this help comes from persons or groups who hold similar priorities, values and views. Through their support, we may come to accept our perceptions as real. We may also find in such persons a source of useful and helpful advice. For example, we might think that a colleague has shown some degree of antagonism. We may then dismiss these thoughts, attributing them to our own problems. A social support person may help us understand that this is not fiction, but reality. The same person might also provide helpful suggestions for mending such relationships.

Community, Commitment and Motivation

Social support obviously brings a sense of belonging and community. When we feel supported, we feel connected instead

175

of isolated. Moreover, social connections bolster faith amidst the greatest disappointments and crises. In fact, as Shawchuck and Heuser suggest, the community often does faith for us when we cannot do it for ourselves.[16] Besides this, community enhances commitment and motivation. A community often finds ways to reinforce commitment to its ideals. Being in community provides occasion to have our flames fanned and stoked by the burning embers of kindred spirits. Without such contact, we become solitary embers whose fires flicker and slowly die. A community can also reinforce finding meaning in our varied activities in ministry. Ultimately, community inoculates against burnout and loss of passion.

Cary Cherniss provides an excellent illustration of this reality in *Beyond Burnout*. In this book, he describes an institution which defied conventional wisdom regarding burnout. All the conditions necessary for promoting burnout were prevalent in the institution, a residential program serving the mentally retarded. The staff worked every day of the week for miniscule pay, and had minimal autonomy. Highly trained professionals shared in the most menial tasks. But, contrary to expectations, Cherniss found no burnout. Instead, he found lively, enthusiastic and contented staff who found their work meaningful and rewarding. What made the difference? This facility happened to be a religious community operated by nuns. It provided a sense of community which, in turn, gave rise to a sense of meaning and commitment, and these qualities served as a buffer against burnout.[17] I suspect this sense of community might inoculate many a minister against discouragement and burnout.

Unfortunately, ministers' solitary habits detract from forming these social connections. We often minimize our need for social supports. Sometimes success keeps us from relationships. Success sometimes contributes to an unhealthy paranoia among pastors and church leaders which makes them wary of others. Sometimes we believe each person around us represents a threat to our position and power. As a result, we isolate ourselves more and more: trusting no one, confiding in no one. I know a pastor who exhibits this distrust of his own pastoral staff. He constantly believes members of his staff are seeking to replace him. As a result, he holds them firmly at bay, suspicious of their every move. Rather than protecting him, this stance has reinforced his feelings of isolation and puts him at greater risk. That's nearly always true. Cutting ourselves off from others represents a serious spiritual and health risk. Constant isolation predicts a slow spiritual death. It also makes handling life's stresses more difficult. Most of us in the social sciences know that persons with social support networks cope better with stress. As such, they can better combat the devastating ramifications often accompanying stress.

The Jethro Principle Revisited

I now turn to the principles derived from Mark 6:30-45. Amazingly, this passage bears remarkable similarities to Exodus 18:13-27. In both passages, we encounter a ministry event involving legitimate human needs. In Exodus, Moses ministered to two million Israelites. In Mark, thousands clamored for their needs to be met. In each passage, zealous servants of God ministered to varied demands while seemingly oblivious to their condition. Moses ministered to the point of exhaustion. The disciples served without realizing their hunger and exhaustion. Time pressures also connect the two experiences. Moses worked from dawn to dusk. The disciples fared no better. Though they were twelve and the crowds were smaller, the time demands were no less real. In both stories, a voice of reason arose in the midst of folly. In Exodus, an unlearned desert nomad corrected Moses' folly: "What you are doing is not good. You and these people who come to you will only wear yourselves out. The work is too heavy for you; you cannot handle it alone." (Exodus 18:17-18 NIV). In Mark, Jesus commanded the disciples with a similar intent: "He said to them, 'Come with Me by yourselves to a quiet place and get some rest.'" (Mark 6:31 NIV). Jethro and Jesus gave similar advice. Both knew that God's servants had to care for themselves if they wanted to tend the needs of others. By caring for himself, Moses would endure to serve others. Jesus did not say this, but the implication is there. Then again, Jesus did not need to say much more. All along He had been modeling what He now taught explicitly. In both Jethro and Jesus, we see a balanced approach to ministry that cares for both God's servants and needy crowds. One last unfortunate similarity bears mentioning. In both contexts, the crowds paid no attention to the condition of these men of God. Israel did not protest Moses' long, hard hours. They kept bringing their cases to him. The crowds huddled around the disciples displayed a similar attitude. They continued to press their demands. Crowds tend to act this way. They often see no farther than their needs. In turn, their needs dictate their demands and their actions. We will wait a long time and perish in the process if we depend on any crowd to remind us to care for ourselves. This doesn't mean ministers will never find sensitive souls in their congregations. In every fellowship, there are persons who see the minister's plight. If we are fortunate, we may encounter caring, dissenting voices offering Jethro's and Jesus' encouraging self-care. Yet, much of the time, people will push their ministers to give more. After all, they pay the minister to do ministry.

Though similar in many ways, these servants of God also differ. This is certainly true regarding both the recipients of their ministry and their ministry focus. However, the most obvious difference is the voice of the one who speaks. Moses had Jethro, a mere human being, albeit wise. The disciples, however, had Jesus, the very Son of God! In Him, they found a loving Creator who cared infinitely more than any relative could. He knew them infinitely better than any other. He knew their frame and fragile humanity. The same is true for us. Jesus still cares for us and calls us away from continual exhaustion. We may refuse to heed the advice of Jethro, but we dare not refuse to hear and heed the voice of Jesus. Unfortunately, some ministers seem to struggle with passages like Mark 6:31 and following. After all, the context indicates a great ministry opportunity: people clamoring for ministers to attend their needs. What a tremendous opportunity for evangelism! What a great opportunity to build the church! Faced with this potential for church growth, many church leaders press pastors for greater effort. They sometimes call ministers to produce more even at the price of their well-being. We see no such demands for overextension in Mark 6. Instead, Christ called the disciples to do less. In this situation, less means more. Doing less allows time to recuperate, recharge and return to ministry with renewed vigor.

Deroling: Making Allowance for the Real You

Jesus' command to come aside in Mark 6:31 involved His disciples temporarily disengaging from ministry to care for themselves. I call this *deroling*.[18] By this I mean laying aside ministry roles for the purpose of self-care. It's important for a couple of reasons. First, clergy roles often carry weighty expectations that can suffocate us. Second, total absorption in ministry can lead us to forget our identity and lose touch with our humanity.

Escaping Expectations

Anyone familiar with ministry knows the multiple expectations which stifle clergy. These expectations define what ministers can and cannot do. They elevate clergy and their families to the pedestal but often the price is a loss of one's humanity. We are often tacitly called to neglect fundamental human essentials: "Don't be a real person! Don't have a life outside of ministry! Don't take time for yourself!" Besides this loss comes the expectation to live like as though we were gods. People expect ministers always to be on call, to be readily available to meet others' needs, and never show signs of emotional wear and tear. Clergy expectations derive from varied sources: from denominational officials, parishioners, family, society and ourselves. Though it may surprise some, Christ does not advocate the suffocating expectations placed upon ministers. He does not endorse self-neglect and self-abuse. This readily appears in His practice of withdrawal from ministry. This stance also shows itself in the text as He calls the disciples to come aside. Though the disciples did not see their own need, Christ did. He called them away from the demands and terror of the oughts to renewed efforts at self-care.

Losing Identity in the Role

Earlier, I indicated that playing a role can lead us to lose our identity. Sometime ago, I read a story about Dennis Quaid. Quaid played the role of the infamous Doc Holliday in the 1993 movie, *Wyatt Earp*. To prepare for the role of this thin, gaunt man dying of tuberculosis, Quaid almost starved himself to lose weight. He was successful. In a later interview with *Best Life Magazine*, he confessed to having developed anorexia.[19] His face and body took on the haggard look of one ready to die. Quaid learned to mimic the gravelly voice of Doc Holliday. He learned the part so well, he began to feel, sense and think that he was Doc Holliday. In essence, he became the role. I read elsewhere that he confessed how hard it was to recover, to separate from the role and become himself again. Most actors know this phenomenon. They know how easy it is to lose one's self in one's role.

The same is true for ministers. Like Quaid, we stand in danger of losing our identity in our roles. That's because there are few professions like ministry. In Christian ministry, personal and professional roles often merge.[20] As a result, we easily come to identify the role and accompanying responsibilities with our identity and confuse our being with what we do. In fact, we sometimes live out of a ministerial persona which estranges us from our real selves. Ben Johnson provides some insight into this dynamic in *Pastoral Spirituality*. He suggests that the minister's role always entails the symbolic role of bearing Christ. However, we sometimes confuse our symbolic role and put ourselves in the place of Christ. In the process of losing sight of our humanity, we can become pseudo-messiahs.[21] Being human messiahs, we quickly exhaust ourselves. That's why deroling is so important. Occasionally stepping back reminds us of our humanity and allows us time to cater to it. That's exactly what Christ desires. He does not want us to forget our humanity or lose our identity through our roles. That's why He called His disciples aside. He wanted them to disengage from their activities and tend to their human needs for rest, food and leisure. One might even argue that this word was the culmination of His modeling. We have already referred to the constant withdrawals throughout His ministry. The disciples had seen this. In fact, they had shared in some of these retreats. What He first had modeled, He now spoke. God is always doing this—modeling first, then speaking. Modeling gives power and authority to the speaking.

Significantly, American Protestants seem to consider the pastor's person a first priority. In the Better Preparation for Ministry Project, people indicated their desire for a combination of personal qualities in their ministers. They noted such qualities as personal integrity, a sense of call, interpersonal skills, spiritual renewal and wisdom. These qualities obviously relate primarily to the pastor's being. They can only be developed and maintained if priority is given to self-care. Only after these qualities did they rank the minister's service to parishioners. Apparently, though they may not always show it, American Protestants know the truth; they know that their pastors cannot serve effectively without first caring for themselves. They also know that the pastor's personal well-being greatly impacts service to the congregation.[22]

If deroling is so important, why don't we make it a regular part of our pattern? The reasons are multiple. Sometimes we fail to disengage because of errors in thinking or negative emotions. We become caught up with the god illusion to the point of thinking we are more than we really are. In the process, we may not think we need to disengage. We delude ourselves into believing we can constantly be on the go without getting exhausted. At other times, anxiety, fear and false guilt keep us constantly in the ministry role. We feel anxious about our own abilities or our security. We fear our people will think us lazy if we take the time to care for ourselves, and we feel guilty if we do. To protect ourselves from these and similar emotions, we stay busy to prove our abilities, or vainly guarantee our security.

At other times, other people prevent us from deroling. Like the crowds in Mark, people sometimes make constant demands even while they see our exhaustion. They are not necessarily callous to our needs; they merely see their own pressing needs and are driven by them. Besides that, we have already conditioned them to think of us as superhuman. Sometimes it's church leaders who make demands that are not humanly possible. Guided by corporate models, they may demand more numbers, more programs and more time.

Even people outside the church may place inhuman expectations on ministers. One minister shared this story with me sometime ago. John served in social ministry. His organization obtained part of their operating funds from a public agency. But ministry proved intense because of constantly serving people with critical needs. Given the intensity and demands, burnout was a real possibility. Over the years, John remained energized through regular contact with a colleague in a nearby city. He obviously needed and cherished these opportunities to derole. John and his friend met on a weekly basis for lunch, prayer and sharing concerns. Both benefited from the relationship. Their time together recharged and renewed them for their demanding ministries. After returning from one of these trips, John received a call from a representative of the public agency. The representative sounded annoyed. He had tried to reach John during his absence. "Where have you been? I have been trying to reach you." "I was out of town. I often visit a fellow minister in a nearby city," John replied. "We don't pay you for that," the agency representative stormed. Apparently, even persons outside the church will not allow the minister to be a real person.

Ultimately, we must hear the voice of God above the other voices which discourage us from deroling. We must hear His voice above the din of errant emotions and people's demands. Amidst the noisy clamor, we must hear the voice of Jesus calling us aside. Then we must heed this call as readily as we respond to the call to engagement. We cannot heed the call to service and yet refuse or distort the call to come aside. *Both* calls come from Jesus. They represent God's call to live a balanced life.

We can help achieve such balance by making deroling a practiced part of our ministry routine. Time spent serving should be balanced with retreat. This is especially critical when ministry has been particularly exhausting. This was true of the disciples. They had spent many days ministering under difficult conditions in the villages. Given their exhaustion, they could not continue to serve effectively or for very long. They needed a respite, however brief, from the demands of ministry. Retreat was not a luxury—it was an absolute necessity. The same pattern should apply to our ministry. Serving others should be interspersed with self-care. We must always move between the poles of personal care and professional functions. In so doing, we demonstrate we are Christians and humans first, ministers second. This twofold movement shows itself throughout Jesus' ministry in Mark. He ministered and He retreated. The two formed the rhythmic movement which characterized His ministry. Surprising though it may be, when we practice this approach, ministry to others does not suffer. Rather, this style enhances personhood and professional practice. To do otherwise invites overload, stress and disaster.

The Principle of Limited Resources

Jesus' call to come aside implies another principle for the practice of ministry. Ministers must serve with the understanding that they possess limited resources. The immediate context highlights physical resources, but mental and emotional resources seem implicit within the text. These resources are always limited. Given this limitation, the many demands can easily overwhelm our finite resources and leave us depleted. We see this in the disciples. They became spent from the constant demands. They needed food and rest. I also suspect that their emotional and mental resources were also severely overtaxed.

Along with the physical and emotional, we may also infer other resources. The disciples possessed faith and spiritual power. For the first time since they had been with Jesus, they demonstrated abiding faith in Christ and the power of His Spirit. This appears most evident in Mark 6:12-13. Through this faith and power, they preached, healed and cast out demons. However, these spiritual resources did not immunize them against the limitations of their bodies. They still grew tired, hungry and needed rest. Beware of those ministers who give the impression that faith and spiritual power make them superhuman. They do not. Faith and power applies to our mission, not our bodies. Faith and the power of the Spirit rarely, if ever, transcend human limitations.

However, the disciples' greatest resource was Jesus himself. His bodily presence must have comforted and strengthened them. Yet, despite His presence, He still called them aside. Christ' presence and power never negate our need for rest and care. I have often heard some ministers say, "Jesus and me equals a majority." By those words they seek to justify pushing themselves beyond their resources. Apparently, Jesus did not subscribe to this view. He was available. He could have resupplied their depleted energy. Yet He did not. He did not miraculously fortify their physical and emotional resources—at least not in the way we might expect. Rather, He chose the natural route; He called them aside to self-care. This path to renewal stands in stark contrast to the method He used with the limited supply of bread and fish. With these mundane things Jesus worked a miracle. Taking the bread and fish, He blessed and multiplied them sufficiently to feed the massive crowd. In the face of human need, Jesus stands ready to work miracles with things like bread and fish. However, when it comes to depleted human resources, He calls us to use the natural means ordained at creation. He does not use supernatural means when natural means will do. He will not perform miracles to cover and endorse the abuse of treasured human vessels.

Limited Resources, Constant Demands

When we ignore this truth and forget our limited resources, we often find ourselves in trouble. It's often easy to do amidst the constant demands of ministry. Some of these ministry demands appear prominently in Mark 6:30-45. They revolved around the pressures the people placed on the disciples. There was a constant stream of people coming and going. Their presence itself constituted a demand. Even if they never had said one word, or made a single request, their presence would still have implied pressure. But this crowd did *not* remain silent. They made demands. One can only imagine the myriad of needs with which they came: "Heal my son!" "Heal my daughter!" "Cast out this demon!" Constant demands! No sooner had one group been served, than another came. The same needs—the same demands—all day long! No wonder the disciples had no time to eat. Who could in the face of this press of human needs? This scene paints an accurate picture of the minister's reality. We constantly find ourselves surrounded by pressing human needs. Constant exposure to and intense involvement with people places ministers at great risk unless we make room for deliberate self-care.

Second, we can infer that the crowds taxed the disciples' emotional resources. One cannot serve under these circum-stances and not be affected. When emotional resources are taxed, emotional exhaustion results. In my dissertation study, I found that over 78% of the ministers in my sample reported moderate to high levels of emotional exhaustion on the Maslach Burnout Inventory.[23] Such exhaustion forms a primary component of burnout. Indeed, it is often the critical doorway. Once entered, burnout is almost assured. The crowd's constant pressures also likely taxed the disciples' energy levels. They were a small band confronted by a multitude. Moreover, they had just completed an exhausting tour of duty. What should have been an opportunity for rest became a new demand to minister and an additional drain on their energies.

One last demand arises in the passage. It's the perennial problem of ministers. This problem involves demands on their time. Apparently it's not a new one for clergy, for Mark makes it clear, throughout his gospel, that Jesus and the disciples experienced this problem. They experienced constant demands upon their time, which made self-care difficult. This appears both in 3:20, and in the Mark 6 passage. In both of these instances, Jesus and the disciples were pressured to neglect their needs by the sheer demands of people and time.

These demands must be taken seriously if we want to do well in ministry. They are limitless in number. They never end. At the same time, whatever our spiritual state, we always minister out of limited resources. No amount of spiritual vigor will erase this reality. Therefore, we can never meet all of the needs clamoring at our doors. This realization should lead us to a deeper dependence on God. It should also remind us that the work and resources for doing ministry belong to God. Furthermore, this reality should force us to implement new strategies: We should set priorities regarding the tasks most deserving our time and attention. We ought to delegate ministry so that others can exercise their spiritual gifts. Most importantly, we should hear the voice of God that calls us to periodic disengagement from ministry. His voice speaks love and tender concern for our well-being. He will not allow misguided zeal or an errant understanding of ministry to make us thrash ourselves.

1. Katherine Anne Porter, *Ship of Fools*, part 3 (1962), from *The Columbia Dictionary of Quotations* (New York: Columbia University Press, 1993).
2. W. L. Lane, *The Gospel According to Mark, The New International Commentary on the New Testament* (Grand Rapids, MI: Eerdmans, 1974), p. 26.
3. F. F. Bruce, *The Synoptic Gospels, The Expositor's Greek Testament* (Grand Rapids: Eerdmans, 1976), p. 32.
4. Ibid., p. 33
5. Marvin R. Vincent, *Word Studies in the New Testament,* Volume 1 and 2 (Albany, OR: Sage Software, 1996), p. 187.
6. Lane, *The Gospel According to Mark,* p. 26
7. Ibid., p. 199.
8. Ibid., p. 209
9. Steve Mathewson, Casey Carey and Dee Duke, "Faces of Change: Three Stories of Pastors Who Grew through Transition," *Leadership* 18:1 (Winter 1997): p. 60.
10. Leadership Editors, "The Business of Making Saints: An Interview with Eugene Peterson, *Leadership* 18:2 (Spring 1997), pp.20-28.
11. Lane, *The Gospel According to Mark,* p. 207.
12. Adam Clark, *Commentary on Mark* (Albany, OR: Sage Digital Library, 1995), p. 617.
13. Sidney Cobb, "Social Support as a Moderator of Life Stress," *Psychosomatic Medicine* 5:38 (1976): pp. 300-314.
14. Dean R. Hoge and Jacqueline E. Wenger, *Pastors in Transition* (Grand Rapids, MI: Eerdmans, 2005), p. 37. The authors noted that pastors who left the ministry listed isolation and loneliness as the number one reason.
15. Ayala Pines and Elliot Aronson, *Career Burnout, Causes and Cures* (New York: The Free Press, 1988). Also Ayala Pines, Elliot Aronson and Ditsa Kafry, *Burnout* (New York: The Free Press, 1981)
16. Norman Shawchuck and Roger Heuser, *Leading the Congregation: Caring for Yourself while Serving the People* (Nashville: Abingdon, 1993), p. 49.
17. Cherniss, *Beyond Burnout,* pp. 182-184
18. Anthony J. Headley, *Achieving Balance in Ministry* (Kansas City, MO: Beacon Hill Press, 1999), pp. 49-56.
19. "Dennis Quaid Says He Battled 'Manorexia,'" http://www.local6.com/news/7965067/detail.html, retrieved 2/19/07.
20. G. Lloyd, "Clergy Burnout," *Church Management* 56: (1980): p. 10.
21. Ben Campbell Johnson, *Pastoral Spirituality* (Philadelphia: Westminster Press, 1988), p. 89.
22. Described in N. Shawchuck and R. Heuser, *Leading the Congregation: Caring for Yourself while Serving the People,* pp. 115-118.
23. Anthony J. Headley, *Personality Characteristics on the Minnesota Multiphasic Personality Inventory and Burnout among Persons in the Ministry* (Ph.D. dissertation, University of Kentucky, 1992).

Chapter 10

Ministry Reframed:
Putting It All Together

Reframing Makes a Difference

What a difference perspective makes! How we frame situations can transform dire circumstances into heroic occasions. That's why life's tragedies rarely destroy people possessing the ability to reframe the events in their lives. In fact, such people often use these situations as springboards for greater growth. Joseph, the ancient patriarch, obviously possessed this ability. He looked at his brothers' malevolence and surprisingly saw the hand of God preparing Israel's deliverance. Sir Winston Churchill, the English Prime Minister during World War II, possessed the same rare quality. During the height of the war, he reportedly challenged the schoolboys at Harrow with the reframe: "These are not dark days: these are great days—the greatest days our country has ever lived."[1] The greatest days? How could he say such a thing? It's because he possessed this marvelous ability to reframe situations. Rather than tragedy and crisis, Churchill envisioned an occasion inspiring and calling forth English valor and greatness.

Reframe has similar power in work situations. It can change the very meaning of work. Remember the illustration from *Tom Sawyer* in chapter 1? Tom reframed the odious task of white-washing thirty yards of board fence nine feet high. This wasn't work. Rather, it represented the chance of a lifetime. So, boys like Ben, captured by Tom's reframe, were willing to surrender their greatest treasures for the privilege of whitewashing a fence. Reframe can promote similar changes in emotions and behaviors as we practice ministry. Throughout this book, I have implied and suggested various ways in which a new frame would make a radical difference in the practice of ministry. From the discussion of the Moses Model in chapters 2 through 4, I have shown how poor ways of framing ministry often produce devastating consequences for ministers. As a means of building a biblical basis for reframe, I have highlighted truths from the creation narrative and the ministry of Jesus. Specifically, I have sought to demonstrate how creation's presentation of human identity implies how we ought to approach doing ministry. The practice of Christian ministry must always seek to remain consistent with the picture of human nature implied in creation. Additionally, I have culled forth principles of creative activity suggesting that these, too, ought to transform the way we minister. Furthermore, I have argued that Jesus' practice of ministry incorporated these principles. In particular, Jesus sought an intimate relationship with the Father through the Spirit as the foundation upon which His ministry was built. For Him, intimacy with God was not an option; it was an absolute necessity.

In this chapter, I wish to pull all of these pieces together by presenting a model for ministry. In its essence, it involves a recasting of ministry as work consistent with self-care as well as other-care. In this understanding, ministry is not simply an other-centered activity. Rather, ministry to others is grounded on self-ministry. It demands a primary place for intimacy with God and appropriate stewardship of one's well-being. Furthermore, such a model does not leave the minister's family out in the cold. It seeks to make time and place to attend to their needs.

Once I have presented the model, I will discuss some of its beneficial aspects. I believe this reshaping of ministry can alleviate some of the stress and burnout ministers experience. In addition, it can influence emotional and behavioral tendencies related to the practice of ministry. Furthermore, this new frame can also shed light on how pastors determine their priorities.

A New Ministry Frame

Given the deleterious effects, I do not think I overstate the facts by suggesting that our current understanding of ministry is a flawed one. We largely function out of a distorted model. This model emphasizes other-care to such an extent as to neglect appropriate self-care and family care. Furthermore, it frequently contributes to a focus on endless activity which leaves little, if any, room for rest, retreat and solitude. In short, it lacks balance. And yet, balance is exactly what we need if we want to do well. All

Christians must find a place for "the mixed life." The mixed life involves a balance of solitude and activity, and frequent movement between the two.[2] Henri Nouwen certainly was right when he penned the words: "The careful balance between silence and words, withdrawal and involvement, distance and closeness, solitude and community forms the basis of the Christian life and should therefore be the subject of our most personal attention."[3] That's especially true for ministers. Balance can be health-enhancing for ministers and can provide a major antidote to burnout. In *Beyond Burnout*, Cary Cherniss notes the following regarding recovery from burnout among caring professionals:

> The most successful professionals sustained a strong commitment to their work by modulating their involvement in work, by striking a balance between work and other parts of their lives. The most successful professionals considered family commitments and leisure pursuits to be at least as important in their careers. They didn't simply work to live, as the burned out professionals did, but neither did they just live to work.[4]

I believe the same truth applies to ministers. To manage stress, to avoid burnout, or recover from it, ministers need to strike a balance in their lives. They need to discover a balanced understanding of ministry which permits them to actually have a life. That's exactly what this model seeks to do. Balance is key. I present a graphic depiction of this model below:

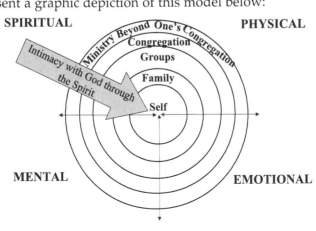

The New Model—What Does It Look Like?
It Is Consistent with Human Identity

In keeping with creation's depiction of humanity, I have deliberately incorporated the finite nature of persons who practice ministry. I do so by showcasing some of the dimensions of human life. Specifically, I have chosen to incorporate the spiritual, physical, mental and emotional dimensions. These dimensions are by no means exhaustive, but representative. They represent some essential areas in which we must guard our well-being.

Ministry also involves relationships. We must relate to God, to ourselves and to others. I depict our relationship with God by the large arrow which shows our intimate connection with God through the Spirit. This relationship is also depicted by the spiritual dimension indicated in the model. Connecting with God is critical to successful ministry: we must experience God's infilling before we can outflow to others. Therefore, we must first cultivate intimacy with God and allow Him to transform us into Christ-creatures. Through the Spirit, we also experience power which makes us effective in ministry to others. But the power springs from the relationship. Intimacy with God always provides the wellspring for power. To eschew contact with God leaves us powerless to perform effective service in the kingdom. So, we must give primary attention to our relationship with God if we want to serve others well. The saintly writer Richard Baxter knew this truth. As a result, he gave this advice to pastors:

> See that the work of saving grace be thoroughly wrought in your own souls. Take heed to yourselves, lest you be void of that saving grace of God which you offer to others, and be strangers to the effectual working of that gospel which you preach; and lest, while you proclaim to the world the necessity of a Savior, your own hearts should neglect him, and you should miss of an interest in him and his saving benefits. Take heed to yourselves, lest you perish, while you call upon others to take heed of perishing; and lest you famish yourselves while you prepare food for them.[5]

I depict our relationship with self and others through the circles which move outward from the center. In order to serve effectively, ministers must cultivate these horizontal relationships. First and foremost, we must learn to relate to ourselves. I suspect the loneliness to which many ministers testify derives from self-estrangement. Having carved out space for self-intimacy, we must learn to relate to our families as a foundation for serving in the world. All other relationships depend on these two inner circles. In my opinion, attention to these inner circles constitutes foundational ministry.

But life and ministry should not remain static. There must be movement. We must become God's active servants in the world. That's why arrows move out from the center in all directions. The center is where we meet God. It's the place where we commune with God and have the life of the Spirit infused into our spirit. Having experienced that connection with God, we move out into the world, beginning with our own household. As Nouwen notes, we move from solitude to community and to ministry.[6]

It Embraces Principles of Creative Activity

I have also sought to include insights gleaned from creation principles into this reframed understanding of ministry. As indicated in chapter 7, those principles include relating through speech, utilizing boundaries, finding balance in one's life and resting from one's activities. All of these are, to some extent, implied within the model. Though there is no logical way to represent speech graphically within the model, communication lies at the heart of relationships. I presume such communication in my diagram. It includes all the varied ways in which we breathe God's life into others through speech. To minister effectively, we dare not omit or underestimate the power of speech.

More explicitly, the model includes a place for boundaries. Boundaries are intended at every level, and demarcated by the concentric circles. Starting with ourselves, we must build consistent boundaries into our lives. We must build healthy boundaries between the "worlds" represented by each circle. This need for boundaries between our worlds may not appear totally logical or evident at first blush. Understandably, we might ask, "Why does a minister need to build boundaries between himself and his family?" The answer is simple. Healthy boundaries permit persons to distinguish themselves from others, thereby protecting relationships from slipping into enmeshment. Those kinds of boundaries are necessary even within families to promote healthy relating. In fact, all human relationships require healthy boundaries if they will function effectively. Without them, relationships become dysfunctional and chaotic.

More evident is the necessity of building boundaries between family and other persons. Ministers have earned a just reputation for allowing all kinds of intrusions to violate family boundaries.[7] This frequently contributes to the "fishbowl experience," where others rob the clergy family of needed privacy. Additionally, ministers sometimes fail to place a boundary around the time given for family concerns. As a result, other concerns often erode family time. The minister may also be so absorbed in work that it makes frequent boundary raids on the family. Even when physically present with the family, the pastor may be preoccupied with ministry concerns. The end result usually translates into emotional unavailability.

In addition to promoting healthy relating, boundaries establish one's responsibilities. This, too, is implicitly captured in the model. It suggests that ministers first bear responsibility to God, then to themselves. Fundamentally, that prime directive involves establishing communion and intimacy with God. But responsibility is not only spiritual in nature; it includes obligations for our entire being: bodily health, intellectual stimulation, emotional well-being and attention to other relevant dimensions. It includes diligent efforts at self-leadership as a primary basis for other-leadership. Having tended to our own care, we are in good shape to tend effectively to others.

Principles of balance and rhythm also underlie this understanding of ministry. That's true at several levels. I offer four observations relating to balance. First, by emphasizing the primacy of the Spirit's ministry to clergy, I suggest that the Spirit's inflowing must be balanced with outflowing to others. Without the Spirit first flowing in our lives, we risk serving from an empty cup.

Second, the minister must also seek to give balanced attention to the varied dimensions of life. Therefore, place must be found for attending spiritual, physical and other needs. The minister must oscillate between these dimensions if they want to experience total well-being. Put a different way, ministers must seek to balance being with doing, work with play, role with essence. Without this harmony, chaos will erupt.

Third, the minister must balance attention to outer circles with that given to inner circles. As implied earlier, these circles represent the varied "worlds" in which the minister moves. The minister who desires refreshment must travel between these worlds, not permanently reside in one. In short, all the worlds need attention and frequent visits in order to promote personal well-being. The pastor who resides in one world alone (usually the frontier world of the outer circles) invites disaster.

Fourth, the ministry of giving must be balanced with the ministry of receiving. That's why the arrows point both ways. Ministers must reach out from a heart filled with the Spirit's love to serve the various worlds they inhabit. But ministers must also allow others to care for them. In this sense, ministry involves mutuality. Too many ministers ignore this aspect of ministry. They focus on giving, but avoid allowing others to give to them and care for them. It's almost as if they are too proud to admit needs and allow others to attend those needs. Within congregations, this happens most often in relation to material things. The church reciprocates materially as the pastor cares spiritually for the congregation. But congregations can demonstrate care in other ways. They can guard the physical and emotional well-being of the pastor who cares for them!

I suspect every congregation has caring souls who see the pastor's plight. They are more than willing to help care for their pastor. They love their minister. They also understand that their spiritual health is intimately tied to their pastor's well-being. Thankfully, I have seen examples of this. Sometime ago, I had the privilege of consulting with the lay leaders of a large church, who were driven by love and concern for their pastor. As a result of that meeting, this church has put in place a program to actively care for all their pastors. Just last year I had the opportunity to lead a seminar for United Methodist lay leaders on how to care for their pastors. The seminar was well attended, and I was gratified to see how quickly these leaders became engaged in understanding their pastors' world. Many were surprised at the difficulties experienced, and eagerly discussed strategies for implementing care for their pastors when they returned home. I suspect if they were more open to receiving ministry, pastors might find that many people in the church really do care.

In keeping with creation principles, there's a place in the model for the "mixed life," where one balances activity with rest. First and foremost, rest comes from *intimate contact with God*. Though intimate contact with God is essentially spiritual, it has marvelous repercussions for the refreshment of the whole person.

Second, rest most often comes when we retreat to our *inner worlds*. By inner worlds, I mean that retreat into solitude in which we usually find rest. In those moments, we have the opportunity to make fresh contact with ourselves. We get to know ourselves anew. In so doing we can separate our identity from our role as ministers. We get an opportunity to derole and be real people. By inner worlds, I also mean retreating into the safety of family. Many ministers act as if family represents a distraction to ministry. In fact, family can often be a safe harbor—an oasis of contentment in a dry and barren land. But family only becomes a safe haven and a place for refreshment if the minister takes the time to cultivate it.

Rest also comes in another inner circle. While I do not have a precise definition for *groups*, the third circle of the model, these may connote networks of people within the church with which the minister relates. One example could be the church's leadership team. But a group might also mimic Jesus' inner circle of three. Within this smaller, more intimate fellowship, He was more open and transparent than He was with any other group. Therefore, groups, in this sense, could include accountability groups where the minister can be real and be refreshed.

It Is Consistent with Jesus' Approach

The model also seeks to remain consistent with Jesus' approach to ministry. As indicated earlier, Jesus followed many of the principles evident in creation already captured in the model. Jesus reserved a primary place in His ministry for the role of the Spirit and intimate contact with God. It's this emphasis that accounts for the arrow indicating intimate contact with God through the Spirit.

As a fundamental part of His ministry, Jesus also made place for *circles of discipleship*. That is, His ministry often started in retreat and solitude, but moved into community with His disciples and ministry to needy people. Henri Nouwen indicates these three patterns of Jesus' ministry in an article based on Luke 6:12-19. First, Jesus moved into solitude. Essentially, this was time given to cultivate His connection with the Father. Second, out of this initial, grounding contact, Jesus moved into community. By community, Nouwen refers to Jesus calling and preparing the twelve disciples around Him as a ministering community. From there, Jesus and His disciples moved out to minister to others.[8] I try to capture this idea by the various circles within the model. Each is a legitimate sphere in which ministry takes place.

Jesus' approach to ministry suggests that it is best done from the inside out. In *Priorities in Ministry*, E. E. Mosley provides excellent reasons why ministry is best done this way. First, circles on the outside depend on circles on the inside. Moreover, the inner circle is where one determines one's priorities and activities. Mosley also noted that the health of an inner circle determines the potential in the outer circles. As a result, if an inside circle is weak, the potential in the outer circles will be limited. One example might be the pastor whose spiritual life is non-existent. This will have adverse repercussions in their congregation. Likewise, difficulties at home will also limit the effectiveness of one's ministry in the church. In fact, Mosley correctly writes that whenever an outside circle takes priority over an inside circle, one can expect trouble.[9]

It Views Ministry as Multidimensional

Ministry in this model involves multi-dimensional activity. That's true in at least two senses. First, ministry occurs in both inner and outer circles. Ministry does not simply involve other-centered activities; it also includes self-care and family care. This understanding is critical to the practice of ministry. Without it we tend to neglect our own and our family's well-being. And, if we don't neglect personal and family well-being, we often walk around feeling guilty because we actually took time to cater to these needs. This ought not to be. We ought to be as comfortable ministering in the inner circles as we are when serving in the outer circles. Second, ministry is not simply about catering to spiritual needs. It's also about catering to the whole person, which includes physical, emotional, mental and related dimensions. That's why feeding the hungry, clothing the naked, visiting the sick, comforting the oppressed and similar activities constitute valid ministry. Biblically understood, ministry has always been to the whole person, not just to parts.

Furthermore, ministry applies to all the circles. Whatever ministry we do in the outer circles is also ministry when done in the inner circles. For example, if organizing a basketball team for community kids is ministry, it's also ministry if the pastors plays basketball at home with his own children. If counseling with someone in emotional turmoil is ministry, it's also ministry if the pastors takes day off for the sake of his mental health. Whatever is ministry in the outer worlds is ministry in the inner worlds. If pastors could get that right, they would save themselves much unnecessary grief, heartache and false guilt.

The Model Is Altruistic, Not Selfish

It might be easy to look at the center circle, see "Self" there, and call this a selfish model. Nothing could be further from the truth! Self-care and self-leadership are always foundational to other-care. Without adequately caring for ourselves, we can never really effectively care for others. Airlines know that. When they give emergency instructions about oxygen masks, they always direct passengers: "If the cabin loses pressure, first put the mask on yourself, and then on others who need your assistance." Even if one has small children, the message remains the same. Those instructions seem selfish, but they make good sense. An unconscious person is useless in such an emergency. In the same way, to fail at self-care makes other-care impossible or, at best, ineffective. Self at the center doesn't always mean selfish. Self at the center sometimes means altruism.

Perhaps we have such misperceptions simply because we do not know what to do with self. Christians tend to possess rather ambivalent and unhealthy attitudes about the self. We sometimes give the impression that self is bad, and that to promote true spirituality we must destroy it. That's because we often confuse a wholesome view of self with the carnal nature. As a result of this confusion, self-hatred almost appears a virtue in some circles. I find this difficult to accept from Scripture. In God's eyes, the whole person is valuable and self is something positive to cultivate, not annihilate. Self does not necessarily refer to carnality. From my perspective, taking care of self is not selfish. Ministers ought to see self-care as an essential foundation stone for serving others. Shawchuck and Heuser were correct when they noted: "The caring and feeding of the pastor's interior life is not an auxiliary to ministry—it is the foundation of ministry. Without this all leadership effort is sterile, without compunction and ultimately leads to boredom and insipidness."[10]

The Model Is Fluid, Not Rigid

Another possible criticism might be that the model appears too linear: it always moves sequentially from self to the other circles in a rigid fashion. That's only true because there is no way to capture variations and fluidity on paper. I intend the model to be fluid, however, not rigid (thus the emphasis on movement). Sometimes ministers will find that a crisis in an outer circle demands immediate attention. In such moments, an outer circle may be given some priority. I find that clergy families understand and approve the shift in priorities when these extreme circumstances arise. It's when they are routinely ignored under normal conditions that they register anger and complaints. Having said this, it's nonetheless true that ministry is normally best done from the inside out.

The New Model: Its Function and Value
The Minimizing of Stress

Ultimately, this recasting of ministry can help solve the problem of pastoral stress. I say this because pastoral stress partly springs from inadequate framing. Stress is not simply a matter of what's out there. Stress also springs from our appraisal of (how we frame or interpret) our situations. If we see our environment as potentially producing threat, harm or loss, we tend to feel stressed. On the other hand, if we interpret the same situation as a challenge, we tend to feel invigorated and do not experience debilitating stress. We call this *primary appraisal*. But stress also relates to secondary appraisals.

Secondary appraisal involves an assessment of our coping resources. Even if our environment has stress-producing potential, this doesn't mean that we automatically become stressed. Rather, we move to assess the available resources for coping. If we deem that we possess adequate resources to meet the demands, we are less likely to become stressed. If, on the other hand, we deem our resources inadequate, we are likely to break out in full panic.[11]

Reframing ministry could help address these issues in two ways. First, by reframing ministry to include the care we give to ourselves and our loved ones, we could minimize much of the stress which emanates from a totally other-centered model. Second, reframing ministry would also reshape our understanding of our ministry resources. There is evidence that we do not fully understand them. The error is usually twofold. For one, we do not always remember that we meet unlimited demands with limited human resources. As a result, we attempt to meet all the expectations of ministry with our own paltry resources, only to find them insufficient. That's a sure recipe for failure! Second, we often forget God as the ultimate ministry resource, and falsely believe it's all up to us. It's yet another example of flawed thinking which invites disaster! Sometimes God has to remind us that it's not all up to us. In fact, God has several others waiting in the wings. And, besides all these other servants, God has His own infinite resources. It's not all up to us. If we would get the facts straight, we could rid ourselves of unnecessary stress and pain.

Avoiding Burnout

Like stress, clergy burnout also springs from a basic misunderstanding of ministry. Roy Oswald's seven-step Clergy Burnout Cycle demonstrates some of these unintentional mistakes. From my experience, I find that this model faithfully reflects the process that occurs as clergy move towards burnout. I provide a synopsis of the seven steps below:

1. The person experiences a call from God and enters ministry with high ideals.
2. The individual finds that there are too many to serve. They find themselves surrounded by a sea of human need.
3. In their attempt to meet these needs, self-abuse, physical exhaustion and unnecessary strain on the family result.
4. The minister experiences feelings of being trapped and of helplessness, and sinks down in despair.
5. The minister begins to develop resentment towards those being served. Their work is approached with sarcasm and cynicism.
6. The clergyperson experiences feelings of guilt and shame because of the resentment harbored toward the people served.
7. Mistakenly thinking the problem lies within, the minister tries even harder.[12]

In this burnout model, I see several framing errors clergy make as they pursue ministry. These cognitive errors, in turn, give rise to all kinds of emotional, physical and behavioral consequences. Allow me to highlight a few of these. In Step 1, I see two potential errors in interpretation. First, pastors often misunderstand the call of God. Namely, they seem to assume that the second call to ministry takes precedence over their first call to live as children of God. This is not intentional, but it happens nonetheless. How else does one explain ministers sacrificing their own intimate relationship with God to focus on doing ministry? As indicated in an earlier chapter, loss of intimate contact with God characterized the wounded ministers discussed in *Spiritual Wholeness for Clergy*. Ministry had become a hazard that jeopardized their spiritual well-being.[13] I have seen the same situation with several other clergy.

Second, one might frame high ideals which are way off-base. Instead of ideals like integrity, intimacy with God and faithfulness, we may set perfectionistic performance standards. We may try to shoot for results which can destroy our humanity in the process. I once interviewed a fellow who maintained such extreme standards for ministry. He projected that within the first five years of ministry he would win a million converts. At first glance, this might sound like a lofty expression of the faith that moves mountains. However, I saw within his statement a standard set way too high. Perhaps my perspective betrayed the paucity of my own faith. Nevertheless, along with others, that's how I saw it. I don't know if this fellow ever entered the ministry. If he did, perhaps he is somewhere out there still trying to make the dream happen, and probably abusing himself in the process.

Sometimes the high ideal might translate into being constantly available to others. I had one former student who projected such an ideal. He was about to graduate and had taken the position of youth pastor at a moderately large church. What's more, he had just gotten married. I suggested that if he pursued this ideal, he would not make it more than six months before he burned out. Not surprisingly, he became intensely angry with me. Three months later I saw him at the seminary. He approached me and thanked me for cautioning him earlier. He quickly discovered that he couldn't live that ideal and do well. Neither could he build a firm foundation for a new marriage. He decided to scale back his ideal in proportion to his human limitations. In fact, he had decided to take the day off and come to the seminary to get away and be refreshed. He was one of the fortunate ones.

Step 2 also begins with an implied error. The novice pastor assumes that God intends for them to meet all the presented needs alone instead of with others. This was essentially Moses' error. He saw Israel's many needs and presumed that he should handle the task alone. It apparently did not occur to him that he should include others in the divine enterprise.

There is one additional error. In Step 7, we find an erroneous framing of the source of the problem. Instead of seeing the problem as one of insufficient resources to meet the demands, the minister assumes that the problem is internal. Maybe they just didn't work hard enough. Maybe they just did not show enough dedication and commitment to the ministry. That's the problem! Locked into this inadequate framing of the situation, the minister misunderstands what is needed. For them, it is not a matter of involving more people in caring for the needs, but working harder! Then the cycle begins all over again. Only this time, the minister renews the cycle with resources that have already been depleted. This situation can only lead to more frustration, pain and self-recrimination.

Once pastors buy into errors like these, they are headed for trouble as is evident in Oswald's model from Step 2 onward. The framing errors evident at Step 1 begin a downward spiral which negatively impacts ministers, their families and congregations. For the minister this often means physical exhaustion, coupled with inappropriate guilt, shame and other forms of self-castigation. The minister's family must struggle with the emotional pain of an unavailable member. In turn, this can generate, within family members, a tremendous amount of hostility toward both the minister and the congregation. Congregations also suffer. They must often deal with a minister who might display depersonalizing attitudes towards them. They might have to deal with many overt and passive displays of anger. Even God experiences emotional backlash when ministers burn out. I have found that, in many of these situations, ministers display vehement emotions—a great deal of anger and resentment—towards God. Nobody benefits from burnout, not even God.

The New Model: Achieving Balance in Ministry

The new model of reframe also seeks to create a balanced approach to ministry. Earlier, I highlighted how the model makes this possible. Here I wish to make a few additional observations about balance—how it relates to our understanding of God and of ministry, the emotions which accompany ministry, behavioral style in ministry and setting priorities.

Corrected Lenses

In addition to correcting our understanding of ministry, this model has the potential to change our views of the God who calls us into ministry. Many ministers seem to envision God as some hard taskmaster who slavishly whips us to produce. As a result, we tend to become perfectionistic, trying to please a deity we implicitly believe cannot be appeased. That's the furthest thing from the truth. God's primary concern is not about our productivity. He's primarily concerned about our intimate contact with Him. That's why everything begins with intimacy, not with performance.

This model implicitly serves to correct another misunderstanding in ministry. Throughout this book, I have repeatedly suggested that ministry is too hard and multi-faceted a task to be done by a single category of persons. Ministry cannot be done by vocational ministers alone. Volunteer ministers must also become involved in the task of serving. Vocational ministers are those ordained persons who serve in the church. Volunteer ministers include everyone else. It takes the whole church to do ministry. This has always been God's design. God has called vocational ministers to equip the church for ministry (Ephesians 4:11-13). Theirs is a specialized task. God has called the rest of the body of Christ to a common ministry within the church. The church functions best when all persons, clergy and lay, find their places of service within the church.[14]

Beyond Guilt and Emotional Exhaustion

Besides changing frames, this model can help alleviate some of the emotional turmoil ministers face. It's well documented that ministers labor under taxing emotional conditions. One of the most prevalent problems revolves around guilt. Ministers often feel their service is not matching up to God's standards and believe they are failing God. They may experience guilt over their own sense of inadequacy in meeting the demands of the job. Guilt may also spring from their failure to give appropriate attention to their families. Many times, these feelings of guilt are entangled with deep resentments and anger at God, oneself, one's family and the church.

Not surprisingly, ministers often find themselves emotionally depleted. They cannot muster enough emotional resources to constantly grapple with all the pain and trauma they encounter in the lives of others. To protect themselves from further emotional onslaught, ministers sometimes insulate themselves. This emotional insulation accounts for the instances where clergy develop depersonalized tendencies towards others.

This model has the potential to address some of these concerns. For example, I believe a great deal would change if we placed a priority on establishing intimacy with God as a foundation for ministry. As Nouwen noted, intimacy with God would create the sense that we are God's beloved purely because of who we are, not because of what we do. As a result, we could give up perfectionist attempts designed to earn God's approval. We would realize that we already have His approval.[15]

Furthermore, knowing God intimately would give us peace about our own worth. We would not need to constantly wrestle with our own sense of inadequacy. We would not need to prove ourselves to anyone. We could stop our feverish activities designed to ensure success and applause.

I believe this model would do much to free us from inappropriate guilt. Having settled on a truer foundation for our acceptance with God, we would not need to agonize over our so-called failures. Does this mean we would become complacent about the quality of our service? Not at all! Quality would now result from a loving, child-like effort to do our best for our Father, all the while knowing that He loves us simply for being ourselves. At the same time, if we seriously considered the two inner circles of the model as places where real ministry happens, we could choose to act differently and give attention to these inner circles. In so doing, we would find freedom from the guilt which often arises simply because we pay attention to ourselves, or because we choose to spend time with our families. Let's revisit the words from my student I quoted in an earlier chapter:

> Putting a scriptural underpinning to self-care has really freed me from a lot of guilt and stress. My wife commented to me yesterday about how different I had been the last couple of weeks. She talked about how attentive I have been to her and the kids and how good that made them feel. What a great moment this was for me. In my mind, I haven't really been more attentive. I have been free from guilt and stress and able to focus on them while I was with them. I have no doubt that translates to the family as being more attentive.[16]

Working out of a new, balanced understanding of ministry would also free us from guilt over our inability to meet every parishioner's need. For one, we would realize that we could not possibly meet all the needs by ourselves. Second, in realizing this, we would likely utilize different strategies for meeting needs. Remember the pastor of the 9500-member church mentioned in chapter 1? He and his leadership team refocused their attention on spiritual direction and equipping the members to care for each other. Now, members turn to these care groups when they are in need. They do not seek out any one pastor to meet all their needs.

Working Smarter, Not Harder

This model invites a different behavioral style. It calls us to move away from perfectionism designed to win God's approval. We already have His approval. Moreover, because of the balance inherent in the model, we can move from an all-work orientation to one which oscillates between activity and rest. We must not be all about endless activity. We must find place in the midst of our ministry for those things which refresh and re-create our being. Ministry must not become a mere exercise in pushing and pulling. We must find opportunities to rest and de-role. Like the disciples, when we have faithfully done what God called us to, we must also hear His call to come aside and rest. I know this call to rest is difficult for ministers to receive. Perhaps it's because we do not trust God enough to continue His work once we have stopped our work. Neither do we believe that, in resting, we are also serving God. Helmut Thielicke, the famous professor of theology was right. He once wrote: "Take my word for it, you can really serve and worship God simply by lying flat on your back for once and getting away from this everlasting pushing and producing."[17]

First Things First

Ultimately, this model invites ministers to put first things first. It establishes a basis for deciding one's priorities in ministry. The priorities in ministry are one's relationship with God, oneself and one's family. These inner worlds constitute important foundations upon which one builds ministry to others. In *Priorities in Ministry*, E. E. Mosley suggested: "When the order of priorities is maintained, greater satisfaction is experienced in a minister's life and greater effectiveness is experienced in work."[18] That's so true! Ministers can never expect to be at their best when they ignore putting first things first.

We may readily agree that intimacy with God ought to be one of our first priorities. However, we may not so easily agree that caring for ourselves and the intimate others in our lives should also carry significant weight. But it should—no, it must! When we fail to pay attention to ourselves and our families, we invariably invite trouble. When we pay attention to the inner circles, we are building a firm foundation for an effective ministry, one which can stand the heat—every spiritual, emotional and physical test— of ministry. In short, we are building the basis for a ministry which will endure.

1. Sir Winston Churchill, from a speech at Harrow School, England, Oct. 29, 1941, from *The Columbia Dictionary of Quotations* (New York: Columbia University Press, 1993).
2. Lee Hardy, *The Fabric of This World* (Grand Rapids, MI: Eerdmans, 1990).
3. Henri J. M. Nouwen, *Out of Solitude* (Notre Dame, IN: Ave Maria Press, 1974), pp. 14-15.
4. Cary Cherniss, *Beyond Burnout: Helping Teachers, Nurses, Therapists and Lawyers Recover from Stress and Disillusionment* (New York: Routledge, 1995) p.162.
5. Richard Baxter, *The Reformed Pastor*, abr. William Brown (Albany, OR: Ages Digital Library, 1997), p. 17.
6. Henri J. M. Nouwen, "Moving from Solitude to Community to Ministry," *Leadership* 16:2 (Spring 1995): pp. 81-87.
7. Cameron Lee, "Specifying intrusive demands and their outcomes in congregational ministry: a report on the Ministry Demands Inventory," *Journal for the Scientific Study of Religion* 38 (1999): pp. 477-489.
8. Nouwen, "From Solitude to Community to Ministry," pp. 81-87.
9. E. E. Mosley, *Priorities in Ministry* (Nashville: Convention Press, 1978).
10. Shawchuck and Heuser, *Leading the Congregation: Caring for Yourself while Serving The People* (Nashville: Abingdon Press, 1993), p. 28.
11. Kenneth A. Holroyd and Richard S. Lazarus, "Stress, Coping and Somatic Adaptation," *Handbook of Stress: Theoretical and Clinical Aspects*, eds. Leo Goldberger and Shlomo Bretnitz (New York: The Free Press, 1982), pp. 21-35.
12. Roy Oswald, "Clergy Burnout," *Clergy Stress and Burnout: A Survival Kit for Church Professionals* (Minneapolis, MN: Ministers Life Resources Inc., 1982), pp. 35-36.
13. Hands and Fehr, *Spiritual Wholeness for Clergy: A New Psychology of Intimacy with God, Self and Others* (Washington, D.C.: Alban Institute, 1993).
14. Melvin Steinbron, *The Lay-Driven Church*. See especially chapter 6, pp. 87-99.
15. Nouwen, "Moving from Solitude to Community to Ministry," pp. 81-87.
16. Excerpt from a student paper. Used with permission.
17. Helmut Thielicke, "Beyond pushing and producing," *Leadership* 16:4 (Fall 1995): pp. 85-87 at 86.
18. E. E. Mosley, *Priorities in Ministry*, p. 16.